Common Sense and Lemon Squares

A Grandmother's Take on Trump's America

Barry Robbins

Copyright and Disclaimer

Dedication

To Pam, my caregiver extraordinaire, without whom this work would not have been possible. Words cannot express my gratitude.

Contents

Preface: A Letter from Mildred

Hello dearies!

I suppose I should introduce myself properly. I'm Mildred, though you probably guessed that from the cover. I've been married to my dear Harold for 47 wonderful years. We have three children—Sarah, Michael, and Jenny—and five grandchildren who keep me young (and keep my cookie jar empty!). My grandson Tommy, who's eight, is quite the handful. Just last week he tried to convince me that "anonymous someones" had eaten all the cookies. The crumbs on his shirt told a different story!

You might know me from my lemon squares (the secret is in the zesting, but don't tell Karen from church), or maybe from my occasional encounters with various important people. I do seem to end up in the oddest situations! But what you probably don't know is how I came to write this book.

You see, it all started one morning when Harold was hiding behind his newspaper (he thinks I don't know about the protest schedules he keeps tucked between the pages). I was making a fresh batch of lemon squares and thinking about everything happening in our country, when the mailman brought a package. Inside was this remarkable book called "NO!"

Well! I couldn't put it down. Here was everything I'd been thinking about, but told through the voices of things we see every day—a hospital in Queens, a Bible in the Capitol, even a right hand that couldn't reach its own heart. Harold kept peering over his newspaper, probably wondering why I was talking back to the book as if it could hear me.

That's when it hit me—maybe I should write down my thoughts about it all. Not because I'm any sort of expert (though I do make award-winning lemon squares), but because sometimes it helps to look at difficult things through a grandmother's eyes. Sometimes a little common sense and a dash of sweetness can make hard truths easier to swallow.

So here we are. I'm going to tell you what I think about each chapter of "NO!"—just as if we were sitting at my kitchen table, sharing lemon squares and common sense. Harold says I'm getting too involved, but then he smiles that smile that means he's proud of me.

I believe in looking for hope, even in troubled times. I believe in speaking truth, even when it's uncomfortable. And I believe that every problem looks a little better after you've had something sweet to eat.

So pull up a chair, dearies. We have a lot to talk about.

With love (and lemon squares),

Mildred

P.S. If Karen from church tells you she won first place for her coconut cake, don't believe her. Some things even my lemon squares can't fix!

Chapter 1

When a Hospital's Heart Broke

On June 14, 1946, at Jamaica Hospital in Queens, New York, Donald J. Trump was born.

****

Hello dearies! Mildred here, and I need to tell you about something that's been keeping me up at night—and not just because I had that extra cup of chamomile tea. You see, I was thinking about Jamaica Hospital in Queens while making my morning lemon squares (the secret's in the zesting, but don't tell Karen from church—she still thinks nutmeg is the answer to everything).

Did you know that on June 14, 1946, at exactly 10:54 AM, those poor hospital walls witnessed something that would change everything? Harold says I'm being dramatic. "Mildred," he said, peering over his reading glasses, "babies are born every day." Well! I nearly dropped my rolling pin.

"Harold," I said, dusting powdered sugar off my apron, "that's like saying an earthquake is just the ground stretching! This was the morning they delivered Donald Trump into the world. Those sweet nurses and doctors, just doing their jobs—cleaning him, weighing him, probably thinking, 'Oh, what a precious little future president!' Though I suspect he was probably already trying to negotiate a better bassinet."

My grandmother always said you could tell a baby's future by their first cry. (She also said you could predict the weather by how squirrels sneeze, so maybe take that with a grain of salt—or in my case, a sprinkle of powdered sugar.) But imagine being those hospital workers! There they were, delivering future teachers and firefighters and good citizens every day, and then... well.

The other day at bridge club, Martha (you know Martha - she's the one who thinks her cucumber sandwiches are "famous") said, "But Mildred, how were they supposed to know?" Well, I just smiled and passed her a lemon square. "That's the thing about history, dear," I said. "Sometimes you're making it and don't even know until it's too late to add more sugar."

Though between you and me, I think they should start putting little warning labels on some delivery room bassinets: "Caution: May Contain Future Threat to Democracy." But then again, Karen would probably just try to blame it on Mercury being in retrograde.

Now, who needs a lemon square while we talk about what that hospital's been carrying all these years?

Chapter 2

When Simple Respect Wasn't So Simple

At President Jimmy Carter's state funeral in the National Cathedral, a photo captured a moment when those gathered placed their hands over their hearts—including former presidents, first ladies, and even Melania Trump. Donald Trump's right hand remained at his side.

****

Hello dearies! I need to tell you about something that happened at President Carter's funeral. I was watching it on television while making lemon squares (Harold says baking helps me cope with difficult moments, and he's right, though don't tell him I admitted that).

You know how at solemn moments everyone puts their hand over their heart? It's such a simple thing. Why, even my grandson Tommy knows how to do it—though sometimes he gets confused and puts his hand over his stomach instead, especially when cookies are around.

But there was Mr. Trump, our future President, standing in that beautiful National Cathedral, and his right hand just... wouldn't move. Every other person there—presidents, first ladies, even Mrs. Trump—they all knew what to do. Their hands went right up to their hearts, like they'd done it a thousand times before. Because they had!

"Harold," I said, nearly dropping my mixing bowl, "did you see that?" Harold peered over his reading glasses and sighed. "Sometimes, Mildred," he said, "the shortest distance isn't six inches—it's the space between who we are and who we should be."

Well! I had to sit down after that. Here was President Carter, who spent his life building homes for poor folks, who never stopped serving others even into his nineties (and let me tell you, I know how hard it is to swing a hammer as one gets older—just last week I helped at the church's Habitat project, though don't tell Harold, he thinks I was at bridge club).

You know, at church social last Sunday, Karen said maybe his arm was just tired from all that golf. I gave her such a look! Even her questionable potato salad wilted a bit.

The truth is, dearies, sometimes the simplest gestures tell us the most about a person. Like when Tommy shares his cookies without being asked, or when Harold pretends not to notice I've been at a protest march instead of line dancing. It's the little moments of grace that show us who someone really is—or in this case, who they've become.

I had to bake three batches of lemon squares that day, just to settle my heart. Though between us, I think even my famous lemon squares couldn't have sweetened that moment in the cathedral.

Chapter 3

When Justice Lost Its Balance

On January 10, 2025, ten days before taking the presidential oath, Donald Trump stood for sentencing on 34 felony convictions. The judge imposed no punishment. The Scales of Justice struggled to comprehend this balance.

****

Hello dearies! Mildred here, and I just have to tell you about what happened while I was watching the news and making lemon squares. (Harold says he can measure how troubled our country is by how many lemons I go through—we're up to three bags a week!)

There I was, watching the news about Donald Trump's sentencing—thirty-four felony convictions, if you can imagine! He didn't even show up to hear the judge's decision. How rude! And the punishment for all those crimes? Nothing at all.

"Harold," I said, wiping powdered sugar off my reading glasses, "remember when Judge Thompson made young Bobby Johnson stock the food bank shelves for a month after stealing that candy bar? What happened to consequences?"

Harold looked up from his crossword. "The scales of justice," he said, folding his paper with that look he gets when he's choosing his words carefully, "work a lot like your kitchen scale, Mildred. They only measure true when nobody's thumb is pressing down on them."

Well! That set me thinking about my grandmother's old brass scale, the one I use for all my blue-ribbon recipes. If I tried telling it that two cups of flour was the same as one, my lemon squares would be a disaster. The measurements have to be honest, or nothing comes out right.

The strangest part? In ten days, those same hands that committed thirty-four felonies would be reaching for the Bible to take the presidential oath. My measuring cups may be just kitchen tools, but even they know that doesn't add up!

Poor Lady Justice, standing there with her scales. I thought about bringing her some lemon squares, but Harold says marble statues don't eat baked goods. Though between you and me, I think she could have used something sweet that day.

Chapter 4

When Tragedy Became Politics

In early January 2025, wildfires besieged the Los Angeles area. Where most everyone saw tragedy, Donald Trump saw political opportunity.

****

Hello dearies! Mildred here, and I need to tell you about something that's been troubling my heart. You see, I was watching those terrible wildfires in Los Angeles on the news, and it reminded me of something my grandmother used to say: "There are two kinds of people in this world—those who see smoke and run to help, and those who see smoke and wonder how to use it."

Well! When I heard certain people (and you know exactly who I mean) start talking about water policies and fish protection laws while homes were still burning, I understood exactly what Grandma meant. Harold found me in the kitchen, just standing there with my wooden spoon in mid-stir, shaking my head at the television.

"Now Mildred," he said, doing that thing where he pretends to read his newspaper but is really watching my reaction, "I can see you're about to say something that's going to make me hide tomorrow's paper."

But he was wrong for once. I wasn't angry. Just sad. You see, I remember when our little town pulled together during the big storm of '82. Nobody asked if you were Republican or Democrat when they needed help filling sandbags. Nobody checked voting records before offering their spare bedroom to a flooded-out neighbor.

The thing about tragedy is it has a way of showing us who we really are. Some people see flames and think about who to blame. Others see flames and think about who to help. It's really that simple.

Though I suppose some folks would try to find a political angle in a rainbow if they thought it would help their cause. Good thing rainbows are too busy being beautiful to care about politics.

(Harold says I'm getting philosophical again. But sometimes, dearies, that's what happens when your heart hurts and your mind tries to make sense of it.)

Chapter 5

Truth in the Dark Hours

On January 14, 2025, six days before Donald Trump would retake the oath of office, Special Counsel Jack Smith released his report concluding that Trump would have been convicted of attempting to overthrow American democracy—if only he hadn't been elected president again.

****

Hello dearies! Did I ever tell you about my father's pocket watch? It stopped working years ago, but it always showed 1 AM. "That's truth's hour," Papa would say. "When all the noise of the day falls away, and you can finally hear what matters."

I thought about Papa's watch when I heard they released the Smith Report at 1 AM. One hundred and seventy pages of proof that a president tried to break our democracy, and they sneaked it out in the dark like a shameful secret.

"Harold," I said, finding him in his chair by the window where he sits on sleepless nights, "remember when Tommy was little and thought if he told lies in the dark, they wouldn't count?"

Harold set down his night-time cup of coffee (decaf, though he pretends it isn't). "Some people never outgrow that, Mildred."

Well! That got me thinking about all the important things that happen in the dark hours. Babies being born. Stars showing their light. Prayer finding its way to heaven. Night nurses keeping watch. My mother always said darkness doesn't hide truth—it just makes it shine brighter.

But here was this report, full of sworn testimonies and hard evidence, being pushed into the shadows. As if 1 AM could make 170 pages of truth disappear. As if darkness could turn facts into whispers.

The strange thing is, they didn't understand what my father knew with his broken watch—1 AM is exactly when truth speaks clearest. When all the day's excuses fade away. When you can't hide behind noise and confusion. When a person has to face what they know in their heart.

I wonder if they thought about that, releasing their report in truth's hour.

(Harold says some folks never learned that darkness doesn't hide things—it just makes you see them differently. But then again, Harold still thinks I don't know about his secret stash of non-decaf coffee in the garage.)

Chapter 6

Money Made of Morning Mist

Days before his inauguration, Trump launched $TRUMP, a "memecoin" cryptocurrency that generated billions in theoretical value despite having no intrinsic worth. The First Lady quickly followed with her own $MELANIA coin.

****

Hello dearies! I need to tell you about something that has me more confused than the time Tommy tried to convince me his piggy bank was having babies. You see, the president has created something called a "memecoin"—not a real coin like the ones in my mother's butter cookie tin, but some sort of computer money that isn't really there at all.

Now, I may be old-fashioned, but I remember when money meant something you could hold in your hand. My father taught me about honest value—a dollar earned, a dollar saved. "Mildred," he'd say, jingling the change in his pocket, "anything worth having is worth working for."

But this new coin of his... well! It's like trying to save moon-beams in a jar. They say it's worth billions, but there's nothing there at all. Even Mrs. Melania has one now. I suppose that makes it a family business, though I can't help wondering if they're selling emperor's clothes by the yard.

"Harold," I said this morning, counting out quarters for the church collection plate, "remember when money was something you could drop and it would make a sound?"

Harold lowered his newspaper just enough to give me that look he gets when he's choosing his words carefully. "Some folks," he said, "would rather sell dreams than deal in reality. Easier that way—dreams don't need to balance their books."

The thing that troubles me most isn't even the coin that isn't there. It's that a president - a President! - is selling nothing at all and calling it something. My grandmother would have said that's like trying to get milk from a rooster—not only won't it work, but it makes you question the judgment of anyone who'd try.

I don't pretend to understand all this modern technology. But I do understand the difference between something and nothing, between real value and wishes dressed up in fancy words.

Though I suppose if you can sell air and call it money, anything's possible. Maybe I should try selling my famous... oh, but never mind about that. Some things should have real substance to them, don't you think?

Chapter 7

Small Courtesies, Big Truths

Presidents traditionally provide military aircraft to transport their successors to inauguration. In 2017, Obama provided a plane for Trump's use. In 2021, Trump refused Biden this courtesy. Now, Trump uses such a plane again for his return to Washington.

****

Hello dearies! I've been thinking about something my mother taught me about manners. "Mildred," she'd say while polishing her good silver, "it's the little courtesies that tell you everything about a person."

I remembered that when I heard about this business with the presidential planes. You see, there's this lovely tradition where the outgoing president sends a military plane to bring the new president to the inauguration. Like offering someone a ride to church—it's just what decent folks do.

When Mr. Obama was leaving office, he sent a plane for Mr. Trump. Before that, Mr. Bush sent one for Mr. Obama, and so on, stretching back longer than my recipe box. But when it was Mr. Trump's turn to send a plane for Mr. Biden? Well!

"Harold," I said over breakfast, "isn't it strange how the same person who happily accepted a ride won't offer one?" Harold lowered his morning paper just enough to say, "Some people think courtesy is something they're owed, not something they owe others."

That got me thinking about young Jimmy next door. Last week, he borrowed my garden spade but wouldn't lend his new baseball to the Peterson boy. When I mentioned this to his mother, she said, "He's still learning about give and take." But you know, dearies, some folks never learn that lesson at all.

Now Mr. Trump is using one of those same planes again, sitting in the very seat where he once sat thanks to someone else's courtesy. I wonder if he remembers? Though I suppose some people have a funny way of remembering only what's been done for them, not what they've done for others.

My grandmother always said you can tell everything about a person by how they treat small traditions. "They're like the stitches that hold a quilt together," she'd say. "One or two missing might not show, but soon enough the whole thing falls apart."

(Harold says I'm getting philosophical again. But sometimes little things, like offering someone a ride or sharing your baseball, tell the biggest truths.)

Chapter 8

When Protection Became the Pardon

On his final morning in office, President Biden took the unprece-
dented step of issuing preemptive pardons to public servants Trump
had threatened with prosecution, including General Milley, Dr.
Fauci, and officers who defended the Capitol.

****

Hello dearies! I need to tell you about a conversation I had with my dear friend Betty while making lemon squares for the hospital volunteers. Betty and I go way back—we were room mothers together when our children were small, though she always insisted on using boxed cake mix (some friendships survive even that).

"Mildred," Betty said, sifting powdered sugar with more enthusiasm than accuracy, "what do you make of President Biden pardoning all those people who haven't even been charged with anything yet?"

Well! I had to set down my mixing bowl. You see, it reminded me of something that happened years ago when our Tommy was little. We knew a storm was coming, and even though the other mothers thought I was silly, I sent him to school with rubber boots and a raincoat on a sunny morning. Sometimes you protect people before they need protecting.

"It's like this, Betty," I said, sliding another batch into the oven. "Remember when you insisted on walking me home that night after the council meeting got so heated? I wasn't in any danger, but you knew some folks were mighty upset about my speech about the community garden."

"That's different," Betty protested, though she had the good grace to blush. "I just didn't want anyone bothering you."

"Exactly!" I said. "And that's what these pardons are—walking someone home before the trouble starts. These good people—the general who chose Constitution over chaos, the doctor who tried to keep us healthy, those brave officers who protected the Capitol—they did their duty. And now they need someone to walk them home."

Harold, who'd been pretending to do his crossword puzzle but really listening (he's sneaky that way), looked up and said, "Sometimes the bravest thing a leader can do is admit they're worried about their people."

Betty went quiet for a moment, the way she does when she's thinking hard. "But pardons are supposed to be for guilty people, aren't they?"

"Usually," I said, checking the timer. "But sometimes love means protecting people from harm that hasn't happened yet. Like sending a child to school with boots on a sunny day. Or walking a friend home when the meeting runs late. Or yes, even using pardons to shelter good people from bad intentions."

The timer dinged, and as the smell of fresh lemon squares filled the kitchen, Betty finally smiled. "Only you, Mildred, could explain presidential pardons using rainboots and cake."

"Well," I said, "some things are easier to understand with a little sugar to help them go down. Speaking of which, would you like to take some lemon squares to that grumpy new neighbor of yours? Sometimes the best protection is just showing people they're not alone."

(Though between us, I made sure Betty took the batch that was ever so slightly overbaked. Some friendships survive boxed cake mix, but there have to be limits!)

Chapter 9

When the Party Moved Indoors

On January 16, 2025, President-elect Trump announced his inauguration would move to the Capitol Rotunda, citing weather concerns. Many speculated the real reason was fear of small crowds at the traditional outdoor ceremony.

****

Hello dearies! Something's been bothering me about this inauguration business, and it reminds me of what happened at the Westbrook family reunion last summer. You see, Martha Westbrook always hosts it in her beautiful backyard, but last year she suddenly insisted on moving it inside, claiming rain was coming. The sky was clear as crystal, mind you, but we all knew the real reason—she'd only sold half her usual number of fundraising tickets and didn't want everyone to see all those empty chairs.

When I heard they were moving the presidential inauguration inside the Capitol Rotunda because it was "too cold," well! I remembered Martha's empty chairs. You see, Franklin Roosevelt took his oath in freezing weather. John Kennedy stood in the snow. But suddenly it's too cold?

"Harold," I said, looking through our old photo albums, "remember when we stood for hours in the January chill to watch President Obama's inauguration? All those people shoulder to shoulder, sharing hand warmers and hope?"

Harold set down his newspaper. "Some people," he said quietly, "would rather look important in a small room than honest in a big space."

That got me thinking about the different ways people handle gatherings. My mother always said you can tell everything about a host by how they treat unexpected guests. Do they squeeze in another chair, or do they pretend they're not home? Do they make room at the table, or do they check your name against a list?

And those poor people who spent their savings on travel and hotels to witness history—now they'll have to watch on television screens at the arena! It's like Martha telling half the family to watch the reunion from the driveway because her living room was "cozier."

The Capitol Rotunda is beautiful, no doubt about that. But it wasn't built to be a television studio. It's meant to be a passage—like the foyer where you welcome guests before inviting them into the heart of your home. Instead, they're turning it into one of those fancy restaurants where the tables are all crowded together so it looks busy in the photographs.

You know what this reminds me of? When my cousin Gertrude used to take pictures of her dinner parties by having everyone scrunch together at one end of the table. The photos looked festive, but they didn't show all the empty chairs at the other end.

"It's about hospitality," I told Harold. "Real hospitality means making room for everyone, even if it means setting up extra chairs in the cold. It means facing your guests in the clear light of day, not hiding behind marble walls and careful camera angles."

Harold just nodded and said, "Some parties are about celebrating together. Others are about being seen celebrating." Then he went back to his newspaper, but I noticed he'd circled an article about the empty bleachers on the National Mall.

I suppose every host has their own style. But my mother also taught me something else: if you have to work too hard to make a party look well-attended, maybe you should be asking yourself why it isn't.

Chapter 10

When Promises Need More Than Words

On January 20, 2025, for the first time in American history, a convicted felon raised his right hand and took the presidential Oath of Office. That right hand had something to say.

****

Hello dearies! I've been thinking about promises. Not the little ones, like when Tommy swears he'll clean his room (though the dust bunnies under his bed are probably old enough to vote by now). No, I mean the big ones—the kind that should change who you are when you make them.

You see, I was watching President Carter's funeral in the National Cathedral. Such a solemn moment, when everyone's hands went to their hearts—everyone except Mr. Trump's. His hand just stayed there at his side, like it couldn't be bothered with respect. And then, just eleven days later, that same hand went up to take the presidential oath.

It got me remembering my grandmother's wedding ring. She used to say, "Mildred, a ring is just a circle of metal until the promise fills it up." I've thought about that a lot lately, watching hands rise for oaths while hearts stay still.

When I was a girl, we had this old Bible at church. Before you could join the choir (yes, dearies, even I was young once), you had to put your hand on that Bible and promise to show up for practice. But Mrs. Peterson, our choir director, didn't care about the hand on the Bible—she watched your eyes when you made that promise. "The truth lives in the eyes," she'd say, "not in the fingers."

I wonder what Mrs. Peterson would say about watching someone's hand rise for power just days after it couldn't rise for respect? Though I suspect she'd just purse her lips the way she did when someone sang the wrong note while looking right at the hymnal.

You know, I still have my mother's cookbook, full of promises of its own—"beat until fluffy," "fold gently," "handle with care." But the real promise isn't in the words, it's in the love that makes you want to follow them. Without that, they're just instructions, not commitments.

That's what bothers me about that oath-taking. The hand went up, the words came out, but where was the love that makes you want to keep a promise? Where was the respect that makes an oath more than just a required performance?

I'm just a grandmother who's seen a lot of promises in her time. I've watched young couples make wedding vows they kept through better and worse. I've seen children promise to do better and mean it with their whole hearts. I've heard deathbed promises whispered and kept for lifetimes.

And I know one thing for certain—any promise worth making should change both the hand that swears it and the heart that keeps it.

(Though between us, I did once promise Karen her coconut cake was "interesting." Sometimes even grandmothers have to ask forgiveness for their promises.)

Chapter 11

A Curious Thing About Bibles

At his inauguration in the Capitol Rotunda, Trump took the oath of office without placing his hand on either the Lincoln Bible or his family Bible, both of which were held by the First Lady during the ceremony.

****

Hello dearies! The funniest thing happened at church last Sunday. Little Tommy was supposed to read from the Bible, but he forgot his glasses and tried holding it upside down! "Well," I told him afterward, "at least you touched it—which is more than some people did at the inauguration!"

That got me thinking about my mother's old Bible. It's so worn that half the gold letters have rubbed off from all the hands that have held it over the years. Even Karen from church handled it once, though she managed to get cookie crumbs in Genesis (which might explain why she's still using box mix—clearly she missed some important lessons).

So imagine my surprise watching President Trump take the oath of office without touching either the Lincoln Bible or his own family Bible! They just sat there in Mrs. Trump's hands, looking as lonely as my peach cobbler at the church social after Karen announced she'd brought her "famous" fruit salad.

"History is meant to be touched," my grandmother used to say, usually right after catching me fingering her antique lace doilies. But she was right—some things are meant to connect us. Like the way every Christmas, we all touch the angel before putting her on top of the tree, even though she's missing one wing and looks a bit like she flew into a window.

The Lincoln Bible has been touched by so many presidents, you'd think it would be as worn as my cookie recipe cards. Though between us, I suspect Mr. Lincoln's hands were cleaner—my recipes have butter stains all the way back to the Eisenhower administration!

I suppose everyone has their own way of doing things. But if you ask me (and I know you didn't, but I'm telling you anyway), some missed connections are like missing ingredients—you might not see what's missing, but you can sure taste it in the end.

Now, who wants to hear about the time Tommy tried to swear on a comic book? No? Well, I'm telling you anyway...

Chapter 12

Now You See It, Now You Don't

Within hours of Trump taking office, the presidential pardons issued by Biden to protect public servants from political prosecution disappeared from the White House website, replaced by "404: Page Not Found" messages.

****

Hello dearies! You'll never believe what happened when I tried to look up those protective pardons President Biden gave out his last morning in office—you know, the ones meant to shield all those good people who chose country over... well, you know. Up popped this message saying "404: Page Not Found," just hours after the new administration took over. It reminded me of the time my grandson Tommy tried to erase his report card from my computer by pressing "delete" over and over. (He still doesn't know I have a printed copy in my cookie jar!)

"Harold," I called from my computer desk (yes, I still keep a doily under the monitor), "those pardons have done a vanishing act!" Now, I may not be one of those computer whizzes, but I know the difference between something that's lost and something that's being hidden. It's like when Tommy claims he can't find his homework versus when he's stuffed it under his bed—one is an accident, the other is, well, let's call it creative repositioning.

The funny thing about hiding things is that it usually tells you more about the hider than the hidden. Like when I make an extra batch of lemon squares and tuck them behind the flour canister—not because they're lost, mind you, but because sometimes a grandmother needs her own private stash. These pardons aren't lost any more than Tommy's homework or my secret lemon squares—they're just being kept where somebody hopes we won't look.

My mother always said, "Mildred, if someone's trying to hide something from you, it's probably exactly what you need to find." Though she was usually talking about my father's Christmas presents, which he reliably "hid" in the same garage cabinet for 40 years.

I suppose nowadays they think if they just type "404" enough times, we'll all forget what we were looking for. But I've been around long enough to know that just because something's hidden doesn't mean it's gone. After all, I still have every recipe I've ever used—kept safe in my recipe box, even the ones some people might prefer to forget.

(Though between us, some things really should stay lost—like my first attempt at lemon squares. Even the local squirrels wouldn't touch those!)

Chapter 13

About That Missing Portrait

Ten days after General Mark Milley's official portrait was unveiled at the Pentagon, and just hours into Trump's presidency, the portrait disappeared from its place among other Joint Chiefs Chairmen. Its whereabouts are unknown.

****

Hello dearies! The strangest thing happened at the Pentagon. (No, I wasn't there personally, though I did once get delightfully lost there while trying to find the ladies' room during a tour. Such handsome young men in uniform offering to help—reminded me of when Harold was in the service, so dashing in his dress blues!)

But I'm getting distracted by memories of Harold in uniform (he still blushes when I mention it). What I meant to tell you about was General Milley's portrait. They had this lovely ceremony hanging it on the wall with all the other Joint Chiefs portraits—my goodness, what a distinguished-looking group of gentlemen! But then, just ten days later, poof! It vanished faster than my chocolate chip cookies at a church social.

"Harold," I said over breakfast, "isn't it odd how that portrait just disappeared?" Harold lowered his newspaper just enough to say, "Some people can't stand looking at honor when it shows them what they lack."

Well! I had to sit down with my coffee after that one. You see, it reminded me of when Tommy got caught drawing mustaches on all the photos in his school yearbook—except he left alone the picture of the teacher who'd stuck up for him when he was being bullied. Even at eight years old, he knew you don't deface the image of someone who chose to do the right thing.

The funny thing is, they can take down a portrait, but they can't take down what it stands for. That's like when Tommy tried to erase his bad grade by ripping that page out of his report card—the grade was still there, he just couldn't see it anymore. Reminds me of our family photo wall—even though we took down Uncle Fred's picture that time he voted for... well, never mind about that. The empty space said more than his picture ever did.

I hear they won't say where they put the general's portrait. Probably in some dusty room somewhere, which seems a shame. All those medals and decorations deserve better than gathering cobwebs. I still have Harold's service photo right there on my dresser, polished frame and all. Some pictures you treat with respect, because of what they stand for.

Harold says I'm getting worked up over a painting, but he's wrong for once. It's not about the painting at all. It's about what we choose to remember and what we try to forget.

Though I do wish they'd at least dust it wherever they've hidden it. A good portrait of a handsome man in uniform deserves that much respect, don't you think?

Chapter 14

About Protection and Politics

On his first day in office, Trump terminated Secret Service protection for his former national security adviser John Bolton, despite ongoing threats against Bolton's life, including a documented Iranian assassination plot.

****

Hello dearies! The strangest thing happened when I was watching the news about Mr. Bolton losing his Secret Service protection. It reminded me of something that happened at our neighborhood watch meeting last spring.

You see, Mrs. Henderson from two streets over (not to be confused with Mrs. Henderson who puts raisins in perfectly good cookies) had reported some suspicious characters around her house. We all took turns keeping an eye out, regardless of whether she'd voted for the current mayor or not! Imagine if we'd said, "Well, Mrs. Henderson, you did criticize the mayor's new parking ordinance, so maybe you should watch your own house."

"Harold," I said while folding laundry, "isn't it odd how they took away Mr. Bolton's protection even though those Iranian fellows are still trying to cause him harm?" Harold peered over his newspaper. "Mildred," he said, "some people think safety should come with a loyalty oath."

Well! That got me thinking about our crossing guard, Mr. Jenkins. He's been helping children cross at Manor and Pine for twenty years, and let me tell you, he's never once asked whether their parents voted for the school board president before holding up his stop sign.

I remember when Tommy was little and our smoke detector started chirping at 3 AM. The fire department came right out—didn't ask who we'd voted for, didn't check our political opinions, just made sure we were safe. That's what protection is supposed to be about.

The funny thing is, I don't imagine those Iranian troublemakers (Harold says I shouldn't call them "naughty boys") are sitting around wondering whether Mr. Bolton said nice things about the president. They're probably too busy with their... well, whatever it is troublemakers do when they're making trouble.

"It's like turning off someone's porch light because you don't like their garden club opinions," I told Harold. "The darkness doesn't care why the light went out—it just knows it has a better chance now."

(Though between us, I did send Mr. Bolton my recipe for snickerdoodles. They may not stop assassins, but everyone needs a little sweetness when they're feeling unprotected.)

Chapter 15

About Doctors and Protection

On January 24, 2025, Trump terminated federal security protection for Dr. Anthony Fauci, despite documented threats against the infectious disease expert's life, including planned assassination attempts.

****

Hello dearies! You know how I volunteer at the hospital gift shop every Wednesday? Well, yesterday I saw something that reminded me of what's happening with Dr. Fauci losing his security protection.

There's this lovely doctor, Dr. Chen, who always stops to chat when she's buying her morning coffee. She wears her white coat like a suit of armor, she says—keeps the germs away from her patients, keeps her clothes clean when things get messy (and believe me, in a hospital things do get messy!).

But yesterday she told me something that got me thinking. "The coat protects me from germs," she said, "but it can't protect me from angry people." Seems she'd gotten some threatening letters because of her vaccine recommendations.

"Harold," I said when I got home, "isn't it strange that we protect doctors from germs but not from angry people?" Harold lowered his newspaper. "Some folks," he said, "think protecting people is something you earn by agreeing with them."

Well! That got me remembering when I had my appendix out last year. That surgeon didn't ask about my political opinions before putting on his surgical mask and gloves. He just protected himself so he could protect me. That's what doctors do.

But now they're taking away Dr. Fauci's security protection, even though some very unpleasant people are still making very unpleasant plans about him. It's like telling a surgeon to operate without gloves because you didn't like his diagnosis!

Tommy asked me the other day why his pediatrician, Dr. Roberts, wears a mask during flu season. "To protect both of us," I told him. "That's what good doctors do—they protect us, and we should protect them too."

I suppose some people think protection is something you can turn on and off like a light switch. But I remember when we all stood on our porches at 7 PM banging pots and pans to thank our medical workers. Seems to me that thanking someone means keeping them safe too.

(Though between us, I did send Dr. Fauci my special "Get Through Tough Times" cookie recipe. Harold says cookies aren't the same as security protection, but sometimes a little sweetness helps you remember that somebody cares.)

Chapter 16

About Trust and Experience

On his first day in office, Trump ordered the revocation of security clearances for 49 former intelligence officials who had signed a letter in 2020 suggesting the Hunter Biden laptop story bore hallmarks of Russian disinformation.

****

Hello dearies! The strangest thing happened at our library board meeting last night. Miss Jenkins, who's been our head librarian for forty years, mentioned she was worried about losing her library keys now that she's retired. "But we still need your expertise!" I told her. "Why, just last week you helped us figure out that mold problem in the rare books section."

It got me thinking about Mr. Clapper losing his security clearance after fifty-three years of protecting our country's secrets. Imagine that—half a century of experience, just switched off like a light bulb because he said something someone didn't want to hear!

"Harold," I said this morning, watching him organize his newspaper clippings (he thinks I don't know about his secret collection), "isn't it funny how some people think experience stops being valuable the moment someone disagrees with them?"

Well! Harold actually put down his newspaper completely—that's how I know he had something important to say. "Mildred," he said, "some folks would rather hear comfortable lies than uncomfortable truths."

You know, it reminds me of when they wanted to replace Dr. Wilson on the hospital board after he retired. Four decades of medical experience, and someone suggested he wasn't "current" enough anymore! Though that might have had something to do with him pointing out that the new administrator's golf buddy wasn't exactly qualified to run the pediatric wing.

The funny thing about experience is that it's like my old cookie sheets—they might not be shiny and new, but they know exactly how to make things turn out right. When Mr. Clapper said something looked like Russian mischief, he wasn't guessing. That's like me knowing a cake will fall just by the smell—you learn these things after fifty years in the kitchen!

Tommy asked me the other day why his grandfather still keeps his old work badge in a frame if he's retired. "Because," I told him, "some things you earn aren't just about doing a job—they're about being trusted to do what's right."

I suppose some people think trust is like a light switch you can just flip off when someone says something you don't like. But in my experience, trust is more like a good sourdough starter—it takes years to develop, and only a fool would throw it away because they don't like the bread it made one time.

(Though between us, I think Mr. Clapper probably knows more about Russian tricks than I know about baking. And I've been baking since Eisenhower was president!)

Chapter 17

When Words Run Out

In an interview with Sean Hannity, Trump made thinly veiled threats to prosecute Joe Biden, suggesting he would use the Justice Department to pursue his predecessor despite no evidence of any crimes.

****

Hello dearies! I need to tell you about something that happened at church coffee hour yesterday. Karen (you know Karen—she thinks everything can be fixed with a casserole) was trying to describe Mr. Trump threatening to prosecute President Biden, and for once in her life, she couldn't find the words. Karen! Speechless!

"Harold," I said when we got home, "what do you call someone who loses a game fair and square and then threatens to have the winner arrested?" Harold lowered his newspaper. "A bully?" I suggested. No, that's what we call Tommy's classmate who steals lunch money. "A sore loser?" No, that's Karen when her coconut cake doesn't win at the fair. "A bad sport?" No, that's the fellow who flips the Monopoly board when he lands on Boardwalk.

Well! The dictionary sits right there on my kitchen shelf, and I'll tell you what—I looked through the whole thing, and there just isn't a word for someone who loses the presidency and then threatens to throw the winner in jail. Even "despicable" doesn't quite cover it. Even "tyrannical" seems too nice.

You know what it reminds me of? That time the mayor's son lost the class president election and his daddy tried to have the winner expelled for "cheating" (which was really just promising better cafeteria food). Except this isn't middle school—this is the United States of America!

Karen says maybe we need to make up a new word. Something that means "so awful it makes your grandmother want to say things she'd have to confess to Reverend Thompson." Though between us, I think even Reverend Thompson would understand some of those words right about now.

The funny thing is, President Biden is exactly the kind of person my mother always told me to be—kind to everyone, patient with difficult people (and Lord knows he's had practice there), always ready with a helping hand or a word of comfort. And here's Mr. Trump threatening to prosecute him for... what exactly? Being a decent human being? Winning an election? Having people actually like him without having to bully them into it?

I did try to find the right words, I really did. But sometimes there just aren't any. Sometimes all you can do is shake your head, say a prayer, and maybe stress-bake a few dozen lemon squares.

(Though Karen suggested we could mail some special lemon squares to Mar-a-Lago. I had to remind her that revenge baking is still revenge... but I did think about it!)

Chapter 18

About Those Pardons

On his first day in office, Trump pardoned approximately 1,500 people convicted of crimes during the January 6, 2021 attack on the U.S. Capitol, where rioters attempted to stop the certification of Electoral College votes.

****

Hello dearies! I need to tell you about something that's been keeping me awake at night, and it's not just because I had that extra cup of evening tea. You see, I've been a poll worker at the First Presbyterian Church for forty-two years. Every election, I sit there at that folding table, checking names, handing out ballots, making sure everything's done proper and right.

When I heard about Mr. Trump pardoning all those people who attacked the Capitol to stop the vote counting, well! I had to sit right down in my kitchen chair. Even Karen from church, who usually has an opinion about everything (especially about my lemon squares having "too much lemon"), just stood there with her mouth open when I told her.

"Harold," I said that evening, "it's like pardoning someone for trying to steal everyone's voice." Harold put down his newspaper completely—that's how serious it was. "Some things," he said, "shouldn't be forgivable."

You know, I remember my first time voting. Daddy took me to the polls, explained how sacred it was. "Mildred," he said, "this is how Americans talk to their government." Now imagine someone trying to stuff a sock in America's mouth while it's trying to speak! And then getting a pat on the head and being told "No harm done!"

I've watched people vote for decades—young folks voting for the first time, elderly people who needed help walking but wouldn't miss voting for anything, new citizens with tears in their eyes as they cast their first American ballot. Every single one of those votes was in those certificates that those people tried to destroy.

Tommy asked me yesterday why we can't just forgive and forget. "Well," I told him, "when you broke Mrs. Henderson's window playing baseball, we made you apologize AND pay for it from your allowance. Some things need more than just 'sorry' to make them right."

The funny thing is (though it's not really funny at all), these folks weren't even sorry! They're still saying they did nothing wrong—like when Karen insists her fruit cake is "supposed to bounce."

I suppose Mr. Trump thinks he can just pardon away what happened that day, like erasing a chalk mark from the sidewalk. But some marks don't erase, dearies. Some things stick to your soul.

(Though between us, I did hear they're serving my lemon squares at the next poll worker training. Maybe a little sweetness will remind everyone what democracy is supposed to taste like—certainly not like violence and pardons!)

Chapter 19

About Our Police Officers

On his first day in office, Trump pardoned approximately 1,500 people convicted of crimes during the January 6, 2021 attack on the U.S. Capitol. Among those pardoned were individuals convicted of violently assaulting police officers who defended the Capitol during the January 6 attack.

****

Hello dearies! I've been thinking about young Officer Jimmy Peterson, who always helps our older folks cross Main Street after church. Every Sunday, rain or shine, there he is with his shiny badge and his kind smile. Last week I asked him why he became a police officer. "To protect people, Mrs. M," he said. "Simple as that."

Well! When I heard about Mr. Trump pardoning those people who attacked the police officers at the Capitol, I thought about Jimmy's badge, about how proud he is to wear it. I thought about my nephew Mike on the force over in Cedar Rapids, about how his mother (my sister Grace) polishes his badge for him every Christmas, just like their daddy used to do.

"Harold," I said while watching the evening news, "how can someone say they 'back the blue' and then pardon people who hit officers with flag poles?" Harold set down his newspaper. "Some people," he said, "only back what backs them."

You know what this reminds me of? Last summer when that young fellow robbed the convenience store and then expected to be let off because his daddy had once helped the owner change a flat tire. Some things just don't work that way. You can't claim to respect the law while pardoning folks who beat up the people protecting it.

I remember when Mike got his first badge. Grace called me crying—the proud kind of crying. "It's not just a piece of metal," she said. "It's a promise." A promise to protect people, to stand between them and danger, to do what's right even when it's hard.

Those Capitol officers kept their promise that day. They stood their ground while people hit them, sprayed them, crushed them—people who now get to walk free just because they did it all in the name of politics.

Every Sunday, I bring Officer Jimmy a cup of coffee and one of my lemon squares. This week, his hands were shaking when he took the cup. "I just don't understand it, Mrs. M," he said. Neither do I, dearie. Neither do I.

(Though I did notice that Karen from church has suddenly stopped complaining about her speeding ticket. Some things put petty grievances in perspective, don't they?)

Chapter 20

An Evening with Betty

On his second day in office, Trump pardoned Ross Ulbricht, creator of the dark-web drug marketplace Silk Road, who was serving life plus 40 years for drug trafficking, money laundering, and running a continuing criminal enterprise.

****

Hello dearies! With Harold away on his fishing trip (though between us, I think he spends more time napping in the boat than fishing), I invited Betty over for a quiet evening. She brought her knitting, I had my lemon squares, and we got to talking about this Ross Ulbricht fellow getting pardoned.

"You know who that reminds me of?" Betty said, dropping another stitch in what was supposed to be a scarf. "My nephew Marcus. Got fifteen years for selling marijuana on the street corner. Meanwhile, this man who built a whole shopping mall for drugs on something called the 'dark web' gets to walk free!"

Well! I had to put down my teacup. "Betty," I said, "remember when Tommy tried to sell lemonade without a permit and got a stern talking-to from Officer Peterson? Imagine if instead he'd built a secret underground lemonade empire and gotten a pat on the head!"

Betty's knitting needles were clicking faster now—that's how you can tell she's getting worked up. "They say he made it as easy as buying socks on Amazon," she said. "And now he's pardoned while my Marcus sits in prison for another eight years."

The funny thing is (though it's not really funny at all), I remember when they caught this Mr. Ulbricht. Right there in the library, they said, probably sitting near those same computers where I help Tommy research his school projects. Though I suppose he wasn't looking up state capitals like Tommy does.

"Six people died," Betty said quietly, her knitting forgotten in her lap. "Six families lost someone because drugs from his website found their way into the wrong hands. And he gets a pardon while others serve decades for so much less."

I noticed Betty had tears in her eyes, thinking about Marcus. Sometimes it's hard to understand why some people get second chances while others don't even get first ones. Though I suppose some pardons are more about who you know than what you did.

When Betty left, she forgot her knitting—that scarf may never get finished now. But she did take home a plate of lemon squares. "For Marcus," she said. "They allow care packages." Some things even a presidential pardon can't make right, but a little sweetness can help you keep going.

(Though I did have to explain to Tommy later that the "dark web" isn't actually a spider's home. He was quite disappointed—though not as disappointed as Betty's Marcus would be if he knew about this pardon.)

Chapter 21

When Simple Truths Got Complicated

By executive order on his first day in office, Trump attempted to end birthright citizenship, claiming presidential authority to override the Constitution's 14th Amendment guarantee that all persons born in the United States are citizens.

****

Hello dearies! With Harold still away on his fishing trip (though I suspect he's really gone to that protest in Washington—he left his newspaper behind, and you know that's not like him), I decided to help out at the hospital nursery. Been volunteering there every Tuesday for twenty years now, folding those tiny blankets and making little caps for the newborns.

Yesterday, the sweetest thing happened. A young nurse, Maria, was showing me a baby girl who'd just arrived. "Six pounds, four ounces of pure American citizen," she said proudly. Then her smile faded. "At least, she is for now."

Well! I nearly dropped my knitting needles. "What do you mean, 'for now'?" I asked. Maria explained about this executive order claiming presidents can just decide who gets to be a citizen, even if they're born right here on American soil.

It got me thinking about all the babies I've seen in that nursery over the years. Some with parents who spoke perfect English, some whose parents needed translators, some whose parents had documents and some who didn't—but every single one of those babies was American from their very first cry. That's what the Constitution says, plain as the nose on your face.

You know what this reminds me of? My mother's apple pie recipe. The ingredients list starts with "Take good apples..." Not "Take apples from this orchard" or "Take apples whose trees have the right papers." Just "good apples." Because when you're making something as important as apple pie - or Americans - what matters is what's right here in front of you.

I mentioned this to Dr. Williams during his rounds. He just shook his head and said, "Forty years delivering babies, and not one of them came out anything but human first and American second."

The funny thing is (though it's not really funny at all), some of those very people trying to change these rules? Their own grandparents or great-grandparents became citizens just by being born here. That's like someone climbing a ladder and then pulling it up behind them.

Before my shift ended, I took one last look at all those sleeping bundles. Each one perfect, each one American, each one proof that some truths really are self-evident—no matter what any executive order tries to say.

(Though I did leave an extra batch of gingersnaps in the nurses' break room. Sometimes when you can't fix big things, you can at least sweeten the small moments. And no, these weren't lemon squares—you have to change things up sometimes, don't you?)

Chapter 22

When Welcome Mats Were Removed

On his first three days in office, Trump issued a series of executive orders declaring a "border invasion," authorizing multiple federal agencies to conduct deportations, and dismantling protections for asylum seekers.

****

Hello dearies! The strangest thing happened at my ESL class yesterday. (Yes, I teach English at the community center—though "teach" might be a strong word for what happens when I get distracted telling stories about Tommy's adventures!)

My student Maria wasn't there. Or Ahmed. Or the Chen family. Empty chairs where there should have been smiling faces. Mrs. Peterson from the office told me they were all afraid to come—something about new rules and agencies being able to pick up anyone, anywhere.

Well! I remembered when I first started volunteering. "Mildred," the coordinator said, "you're not just teaching English. You're teaching welcome." I thought she meant making people feel comfortable with irregular verbs (which, between us, I'm not always comfortable with myself).

You know what this reminds me of? Last Thanksgiving, when I accidentally locked the front door while all the pies were cooling on the windowsill. There were my children and grandchildren, standing out in the cold, watching those pies through the window! That's what these new rules feel like—keeping people on the outside, looking in at everything they helped make.

I tried calling Maria to check on her family. Her little boy Mateo answered—he's in Tommy's class, you know. "Mrs. M," he said in perfect third-grade English, "Mama says we have to be careful now." Imagine that—a child having to translate fear for his mother.

The funny thing is (though it's not really funny at all), my own grandmother used to tell stories about coming through Ellis Island. "They checked our eyes, our papers, our pockets," she'd say, "but never our hearts. America was smart enough to know that hope makes the best citizens."

After class (a very quiet class), I went to put up next week's lesson plans. Found myself just staring at the Statue of Liberty poster on the wall. Below it someone had written "Give me your tired, your poor..." in wobbly English letters—Maria's handwriting, I think.

I left the lesson plans blank. Somehow, conjugating verbs doesn't seem as important as conjugating kindness these days.

(Though I did leave a plate of snickerdoodles by every empty chair. Sometimes a cookie is more than a cookie—it's a promise to save someone's seat until they can come back. And no, not lemon squares this time—Maria always said snickerdoodles reminded her of her grandmother's cookies back home. Wherever home is, it should smell like something sweet, don't you think?)

Chapter 23

When Papers Changed But People Didn't

On his first day in office, Trump ordered all federal agencies to reverse gender marker changes on identification documents, forcing transgender Americans' official IDs to reflect their sex assigned at birth.

****

Hello dearies! Harold's home from his "fishing trip," and while I was making him welcome-home lemon squares, we got to talking about this business with federal identification papers.

You see, when our Sarah was little, she tried to write "princess" as her occupation on her library card application. The librarian just smiled and said, "Honey, what's in your heart doesn't always get to go on paper." Well! Now the government's doing the same thing to transgender folks—telling them their federal papers can't match what's in their hearts.

"Harold," I said, sifting powdered sugar maybe a bit too vigorously, "remember when they made us change all our paperwork that time the bank insisted my middle name was Jane instead of

June? Took three months to fix, and I was the same person the whole time."

Harold set down his newspaper. "Difference is, Mildred, you got to change your papers to match who you are. They're making people change their papers to match who they aren't."

My grandmother had a saying about truth: "You can write 'sugar' on a salt shaker, but that won't make the biscuits any sweeter." Seems to me changing someone's passport or Social Security card doesn't change who they are—it just makes life harder every time they have to show those papers.

I've been rolling that thought around like sugar on a lemon square. Sometimes the simplest truths are like my best recipes—you can't improve them by complicating things that ought to be simple.

(Though I did notice my lemon squares disappeared extra quickly at the post office today. Sometimes people need a little sweetness when the world's being sour.)

Chapter 24

When Safe Places Weren't

On January 24, 2025, Trump ordered all transgender women in federal prisons to be transferred to men's facilities, where statistics show they are ten times more likely to be sexually assaulted.

****

Hello dearies! I need to tell you about something that happened at our church daycare center yesterday. Little Tommy's friend Madison was crying because they were renovating her usual classroom, and she had to move to the boys' room temporarily. "But I don't belong there," she kept saying. "That's not my safe place."

It got me thinking about what I'd just read in the newspaper about transgender women in federal prisons being moved to men's facilities. My heart just about broke, thinking of those women being sent somewhere they know isn't safe for them.

"It's about proper placement," some official said on TV. Well! That reminded me of the time Karen insisted that fruit pies had to go on the "pastry" table at the church social just because they had crust, even though everyone knows they belong with the other fruit dishes. Sometimes people get so caught up in their categories that they forget about what makes sense.

I volunteer at the county jail's library (yes, even jails have libraries—people need books everywhere, though Karen thinks we should only send them cookbooks so they can "learn a useful skill"). There's this guard, Officer Martinez, who's been there twenty years. "You know what I've learned, Mrs. M?" she told me. "Safety isn't about rules—it's about putting people where they can stay whole."

My grandmother used to say that being safe isn't just about having a roof over your head—it's about being somewhere your heart can rest. I've been thinking about that while making this morning's lemon squares. About how some things are so simple that only humans could complicate them.

(Though between us, when Tommy heard about Madison's situation, he offered to let her share his special corner in the other classroom. Sometimes children understand things better than all the officials in Washington.)

Chapter 25

When Life and Death Got Simpler

On his first day in office, Trump issued an executive order to expand the death penalty, directing the Justice Department to pursue capital punishment more aggressively and help states obtain execution drugs and carry out more executions.

****

Hello dearies! Something's been weighing on my mind since choir practice yesterday. You see, we were singing "Amazing Grace" when Mrs. Peterson mentioned her brother—he's been a prison chaplain for forty years. What he told her about these new orders to speed up executions just stopped my voice mid-hymn.

"The thing is, Mildred," she said afterward while we were putting away the hymnals, "they're treating it like it's just paperwork. Like checking boxes on a form."

Well! That reminded me of the time Karen tried to speed up her bread-making by turning up the oven temperature. "Higher heat means faster baking," she said. But you can't rush some things without ruining them completely—and Karen's charred loaves proved that better than any sermon could.

I mentioned this to Harold over breakfast. "Some decisions," he said, looking up from his newspaper, "need to take exactly as long as they take." He was a jury foreman once, you know. Spent three weeks deliberating a shoplifting case because "getting it right matters more than getting it done."

The funny thing about time is how differently we treat it. We'll spend hours debating whether my lemon squares need more zest (they don't, no matter what Karen says), but now they want to hurry through decisions about life and death? My grandmother would have something to say about that kind of math.

Tommy asked me yesterday why his homework had to be "exactly right" when he could get it done faster by guessing. I told him some things are too important for guessing. Some answers need to be certain.

(Though I did have to explain to Karen that comparing her rushed meatloaf to rushed justice wasn't quite the same thing. Even if both decisions could be considered matters of life and death, depending on who's doing the cooking.)

Chapter 26

When Neighbors Needed Neighbors

While touring hurricane damage in North Carolina, Trump announced he was considering "getting rid of" FEMA, suggesting states should handle their own disasters without federal help.

****

Hello dearies! I was having tea with Betty yesterday when I nearly spilled my cup all over her knitting (that poor scarf she's been working on since last Christmas still looks more like a pot holder). You see, she'd just told me the president wants to get rid of FEMA completely. Let states handle their own disasters, he says.

Well! I haven't been this worked up since Tommy tried to convince me that throwing his vegetables to the dog counted as "recycling."

"Betty," I said, probably a bit too loudly, "remember the flood of '87? When half the state was underwater?" I watched her face change as she remembered. How the water just kept rising. How our little church basement shelter quickly ran out of everything.

How we were standing there in rising water, running out of hope, when those FEMA trucks finally rolled in.

"It's like someone watching their neighbor's house burn down and saying 'Well, they should have bought a better garden hose,'" I told Harold later. He lowered his newspaper just enough to say, "Some people don't believe in helping until they need help themselves."

You know what this reminds me of? When Tommy's school principal suggested each class should handle their own fire drills. Just think about that for a minute. Third-graders in charge of evacuation plans! Though between us, they probably would have done a better job than some folks in Washington.

The thing about disasters is they don't send appointment cards. They don't check your bank account or your state budget before deciding where to strike. Mississippi's levees don't care if Mississippi can afford to fix them. California's fires don't stop to ask if California has enough fire trucks.

Betty set down her knitting (that scarf wasn't getting any better anyway) and said, "You know what really gets me? The same folks who want to get rid of FEMA probably have premium insurance on their vacation homes."

(Though I did have to take a breath and remind myself that getting mad doesn't fix things. But sometimes, dearies, it's okay to let your lemon squares have a little extra bite to them.)

Chapter 27

When Bills Started Looking Like Ransom Notes

Within 48 hours of taking office, Trump signed executive orders dismantling healthcare protections and subsidies, threatening coverage for over 20 million Americans.

****

Hello dearies! I've been sitting here at my kitchen table for an hour, staring at a letter from my friend Alice at the hospital billing office. She's worked there thirty years, and I've never heard her sound so upset.

"Mildred," she said, her voice shaking, "they're taking away people's health coverage like it's just paperwork. Twenty million people! Do you know what those numbers look like from where I sit? I'm already seeing the collection notices piling up on my desk."

Well! That reminded me of when Tommy had his appendix out last year. The bill came to $45,000—more than Harold and I paid for our first house! Thank heaven for insurance. But now they're talking about stripping away protections, dropping subsidies, letting insurance companies go back to calling everything a "pre-existing condition."

"It's like they think people get sick on purpose," I told Harold over breakfast. He set down his newspaper completely—that's how you know something's serious. "Some folks," he said, "think health is something you earn, like a merit badge at scout camp."

You know what this reminds me of? When our church tried saving money by canceling the roof repair fund. "We'll fix leaks as they happen," they said. Three months later, we were holding services with umbrellas, and the repair bill was triple what it would have been.

The numbers Alice showed me just about stopped my heart. $75,000 for a premature birth. $150,000 for cancer treatment. And now they're planning to pull the safety net out from under families already walking a tightrope.

"But what can we do?" Alice asked, showing me stack after stack of bills that would ruin families who are just trying to stay alive.

I thought about my grandmother's button jar—how she saved every spare button "just in case." She understood something these folks in Washington don't: you don't wait until someone's shirt is falling apart to make sure you have buttons.

(Though I did have to take a plate of lemon squares down to Alice's office. Not because they'd help with those astronomical bills, but because sometimes when you can't fix the big things, you at least let people know they're not facing them alone.)

A Letter from Cousin Maria

Hello dearies! I've been sitting here at my kitchen table for over an hour, reading and re-reading this letter that just arrived from my cousin Maria in Hungary. My hands are shaking so badly I've had to make three attempts at my lemon squares, and you know that recipe is as familiar to me as breathing.

"Harold," I said, probably a bit too loudly, "Maria's written to us. Remember that summer evening you taught us to catch fireflies before her family moved back to Hungary?"

Harold set down his newspaper completely—that's how I knew this was serious. We sat there together, reading Maria's words about what happened to her country. About how democracy can slip away so quietly you hardly notice until it's too late. About how the path her country took looks so familiar now.

I keep thinking about those summers we shared as girls, when everything seemed possible and the worst thing we could imagine was running out of cookie dough. Now here's Maria, trying to warn us about where our own path might lead.

I think you need to read this letter for yourselves. Some things are too important not to share.

****

My dearest cousin Mildred,

I've been thinking about those summers we spent together as girls, before my family returned to Hungary. Remember how we would sit in your mother's kitchen, sharing secrets and sneaking bits of cookie dough? You always said your lemon squares would never be as good as Aunt Sarah's. (Though now, I suspect you've long surpassed her—don't tell her I said that!)

But Mildred, what I'm seeing in American newspapers these days makes my hands shake so badly I can hardly hold my morning coffee. It's like watching a newsreel from our past playing out in your present.

It started here so slowly that most people didn't notice. Like how water can wear away stone—not in drops, but in years. First, Orbán began talking about "real Hungarians" and who truly belonged. It reminded me of how old Mrs. Kovács used to sort her garden vegetables—these are perfect for Sunday dinner, these for everyday soup, these... well, these don't belong at all.

Then the changes came faster. The newspaper my István had written for since university suddenly had new owners. "Nothing will change," they said. But within months, reporters who asked difficult questions found themselves covering local cat shows instead of parliament. Now we have newspapers, of course—they're just all singing from the same song sheet, like that awful church choir when Sister Agnes insisted on conducting.

Remember how we used to argue about whose grandmother made better strudel? We could disagree but still share the pastries.

Now, in my weekly coffee group, we've learned to watch what we say. Sweet Mrs. Német spoke up last month about her son losing his teaching position for using the "wrong" textbooks. The next week, her grandson's university application was mysteriously "lost."

The courts changed too. One by one, like lights going out in a house at night. Each time, they appointed "more reliable" judges. Strange, isn't it, how reliability came to mean something different than what our mothers taught us?

Do you recall that summer we got lost picking blackberries and convinced ourselves we could find new paths home? How everything familiar suddenly looked different? That's what it feels like now—except the paths don't lead back home anymore.

Yesterday, my granddaughter asked me why her friend's family was moving to Germany. How do you explain to a child that her friend's mother, a judge for twenty years, can no longer bear to deliver verdicts that have been decided before she enters the courtroom?

They still call us a democracy. We still have elections. But Mildred, it's like those fake cakes in the bakery window—they look perfect until you realize they're made of plastic. Our parliament building still stands proud, but inside it's become a theater where all the lines have been written in advance.

I see your Mr. Trump talking about "disloyal" judges and "enemy" journalists, about who is and isn't a "real" American. Oh, Mildred, it's like hearing an echo of our past in your present.

You know what frightens me most? Not the big dramatic changes—those at least wake people up. It's the small surrenders. The moment you decide it's easier not to mention politics at dinner. The day you find yourself adding "of course" after "yes" just a bit too quickly. The morning you realize you're proud of your children for learning to keep their thoughts to themselves.

I'm writing this letter sitting in my kitchen, looking out at my garden where the morning glories still bloom every dawn, whether the government approves or not. Nature, at least, doesn't bow to authoritarians. But I worry, dear cousin. I worry when I see your country starting down the same path we took, one small step at a time.

They tell us Hungary is stronger now. More stable. More "traditional." Perhaps. But strength built on fear isn't strength at all—rather like those tomato plants my mother used to tie too tightly to their stakes. They stood straight, yes, but they never grew quite right.

Please, share this letter if you think it will help. Let people know that democracy doesn't usually die in a single moment. It fades, like a photograph left in the sun, until one day you can barely recognize what it once showed.

Give my love to Harold. Tell him I still remember how he taught us to catch fireflies that summer evening when everything seemed possible.

With all my love and worry,

Your cousin Maria

P.S. I'm enclosing my strudel recipe—the real one, not the one I used to claim was authentic. Some truths shouldn't wait until it's too late to share them.

****

Well! I've had to sit down again after reading it one more time. Harold hasn't said a word, but he's been staring at the same page of his newspaper for an hour.

The thing about warnings is that they only help if you heed them. Rather like how Tommy had to learn about hot stoves the hard way, no matter how many times we told him.

Though I suppose some lessons are too important to learn the hard way.

(And yes, I'm going to try Maria's strudel recipe. Some connections need to be kept alive, especially now.)

Chapter 28

When Home Became Real Estate

After suggesting Egypt and Jordan take in Gaza's 2.3 million Palestinians, one cannot help but recall Trump's previous promotion of his vision of transforming the territory into a luxury resort "better than Monaco," built on ethnically cleansed land.

****

Hello dearies! I need to tell you about something that happened at our community garden yesterday. Mr. Cohen, who's tended his tomato patch there for thirty years, came to me almost in tears. Someone had suggested turning our little garden into a parking lot for the new shopping center.

"But this is more than just dirt and vegetables," he told me, his hands still covered in the soil he loves. "This is where my father taught me to plant. Where my children learned to grow things. Where our community comes together."

Well! It got me thinking about what I'd just read in the paper—about plans to turn Gaza into some kind of luxury resort.

Just clear out all those families, wipe away their homes and histories, and build something "better than Monaco," they say.

"Harold," I said while mixing a batch of lemon squares (my hands needed something to do before they turned into fists), "remember when that developer wanted to turn the old Peterson place into 'luxury condos'? Said he'd make it 'better than anything this town had ever seen'?"

Harold looked up from his newspaper. "Funny how some folks think anything can be improved by adding the word 'luxury' to it," he said. Then added, quietly, "Even if it means erasing what was there before."

You know what this reminds me of? When Tommy was little, he decided to "improve" his sister's dollhouse by turning it into a garage for his toy cars. "But it'll be a really nice garage!" he said, not understanding why his sister was crying. Some things mean more to people than just the space they take up.

I've been thinking about what "better" really means. Better than memories of your grandmother's kitchen? Better than the olive trees your great-grandfather planted? Better than the streets where your children took their first steps?

The community garden is safe, by the way. Turns out even luxury parking lots need someone's approval. Though I notice the developer never asked the gardeners what they thought about his "improvement" plans.

(Though I did leave an extra plate of cookies in the garden shed. Sometimes people need a reminder that the sweetest things in life aren't bought—they're grown, tended, and passed down through generations.)

Chapter 29

When Prayer Became Politics

At the traditional National Cathedral prayer service following his inauguration, Trump demanded an apology from the Episcopal bishop who asked him to "have mercy" on LGBTQ+ people and migrants, calling her a "so-called Bishop" and her service "boring and uninspiring."

****

Hello dearies! Something happened at church coffee hour that I just can't stop thinking about. Karen (you remember Karen—she thinks adding raisins to everything makes it "fancy") was going on about how "inappropriate" it was for that Episcopal bishop to pray for mercy for immigrants and LGBTQ+ folks during the National Cathedral service.

"Politics doesn't belong in church," she declared, adjusting her "Make America Great Again" pin on her Sunday best.

Well! I haven't been that speechless since Tommy tried to convince me that chocolate chip cookies counted as breakfast because they had eggs in them.

"Karen," I said, as gently as I could manage, "isn't asking for mercy exactly what we're supposed to do in church?" She looked at me like I'd suggested we replace the hymnal with rock and roll.

Harold, who usually stays out of church discussions (he says one opinionated Methodist in the family is enough), actually spoke up. "Funny how some folks think prayer is only appropriate when it matches their politics."

You know what this reminds me of? When our old Reverend Thompson prayed for peace during Vietnam, and half the congregation walked out. He just kept right on praying. "God's house," he told me later, "is big enough for uncomfortable truths."

The funny thing is, Karen had no problem when our church prayed for her nephew's "lifestyle choices" (he bought a motorcycle). But pray for mercy for people seeking refuge? Suddenly that's "too political."

"I just don't think the National Cathedral is the place for such controversial topics," Karen sniffed.

"Where better?" I asked. "If we can't pray for mercy in a cathedral, should we do it in the parking lot? Behind the Piggly Wiggly, maybe?"

(Though I did notice Karen skipped the "pray for your enemies" part of the service. Some prayers are harder to swallow than others—rather like her raisin-studded potato salad.)

Chapter 30

When Help Got Put On Hold

On January 27, 2025, Trump's Office of Management and Budget ordered an immediate freeze on virtually all federal financial assistance, threatening billions in aid to Americans.

****

Hello dearies! I've been sitting here at my kitchen window, watching the road crews try to fix that big sinkhole on Maple Street. Or at least, they were fixing it until yesterday. Now there's just a bunch of orange cones around a hole that keeps getting bigger.

"Budget freeze," the foreman told me when I brought out some coffee. "Everything stops until further notice." He looked at that growing hole like it was personally offending him. "Twenty-three years on the job," he said, "and I've never had to just walk away from a hazard before."

Well! When Harold showed me the news about stopping all federal assistance, I thought about that hole on Maple Street. About the school lunch program Tommy's friend depends on. About the senior center's Meals on Wheels that Betty helps deliver. About all these pieces of help that people count on, suddenly frozen like somebody pulled the plug on caring.

"It's like turning off the heat to save money," I told Harold, "and then acting surprised when the pipes freeze."

Harold set down his newspaper. "Some folks," he said, "think you can just press pause on people's needs."

You know what this reminds me of? When our church decided to save money by turning off the water fountain. Didn't think about old Mrs. Jenkins who needs water for her heart pills, or the Sunday school children after their games. Sometimes saving pennies costs more than dollars.

The foreman says that sinkhole's getting wider every day they can't work on it. Rather like problems do when you decide to stop fixing them. Though I suppose if you live in a nice enough neighborhood, you can always drive around the holes.

I ran into Betty at the grocery store. She was trying to figure out how to tell her Meals on Wheels folks that their food might stop coming. "Maybe they can just eat less," she said, her voice sharp with sarcasm. "Like hunger takes a holiday when budgets do."

(Though I notice the country club across town just got approved for new golf carts. Funny how some kinds of spending never seem to freeze.)

Chapter 31

When Water Got Patriotic

In his inaugural address, President Trump announced he would rename the Gulf of Mexico as the Gulf of America.

****

Hello dearies! The most ridiculous thing happened at our garden club meeting yesterday. Tommy had made a lovely presentation about the class fish tank he's responsible for this week (though between us, those fish look awfully nervous about his enthusiasm). Afterward, someone mentioned the news about renaming the Gulf of Mexico.

"They want to call it what?" I asked, nearly dropping my pruning shears. "The Gulf of America?"

Well! That reminded me of the time Tommy tried to rename our cat "Super Tommy's Amazing Tiger" because he thought "Whiskers" wasn't grand enough. Whiskers, I should mention, was distinctly unimpressed by this attempt at rebranding.

"Harold," I said later, while he was pretending to do his crossword puzzle, "do you suppose the fish care what we call their water?"

Harold lowered his newspaper just enough to say, "Some folks think putting their name on something makes it theirs. Rather like when Tommy wrote his name on all the cookies."

You know what this reminds me of? When our new mayor tried to rename Main Street after himself. Old Mrs. Wilson, who's lived there ninety-three years, just kept addressing her Christmas cards with the old name. "Geography," she told me, "has a longer memory than politicians."

I mentioned this at bridge club, and Betty (still working on that eternal scarf) said, "What's next? The Pacific Ocean becomes the Patriotic Ocean? The Rocky Mountains become the Really American Mountains?"

The funny thing is, I've been baking pies longer than most folks have been alive, and I've never once had to rename an apple to make it taste better. Though I suppose if you can't actually fix things, you can always try calling them something else.

(Though I notice they didn't ask Mexico what they thought about this nautical name change. Rather like when Tommy renamed Whiskers without consulting the cat.)

Chapter 32

A Little Visit to Greenland

On his first day in office, Trump renewed his interest in acquiring Greenland, claiming Denmark "can't maintain it" and citing Russian and Chinese threats to "international security."

****

Hello dearies! When I heard the president wanted to buy Greenland (again!), I told Harold we simply had to go see for ourselves. "Now Mildred," he said, adjusting his winter hat, "most people just write letters." But you know me—and somehow Karen from church got wind of it and insisted on coming along. (She told everyone she was bringing her "world-famous" casserole. Those poor Greenlanders!)

Well! The loveliest people you'd ever want to meet. They just laughed when I asked if they were for sale. "Would you sell your home just because someone thinks they can maintain it better?" their elder asked me. That got me thinking about the time our neighbor Mr. Peterson offered to "help maintain" our garden. I told him the same thing my grandmother always said: "Just because someone thinks they can run your life better doesn't mean they should."

The Greenlanders insisted we try their traditional whale blubber (Harold turned a fascinating shade of green), and in return, I taught them to make lemon squares. Though finding fresh lemons that far north was quite an adventure! Karen kept suggesting they use canned filling, but some things you just don't compromise on.

During our baking class, one of the ladies told me something I'll never forget. "Our land isn't real estate," she said, sifting flour like she'd been doing it all her life. "It's our heritage, our future, our identity." Well! That reminded me of when developers wanted to buy our church's community garden to build a parking lot. Some things aren't for sale because their value isn't about money at all.

Harold, who'd finally got his color back, said it was like trying to buy someone's family photo album—even if you could afford it, that's not really the point, is it?

(Karen spent the whole trip trying to convince them that her casserole would be perfect for "tourist restaurants." But some things are better left in their natural state—like Greenland, and possibly Karen's cooking.)

You know, watching the northern lights dance over all that ancient ice, I couldn't help but think: some folks see the world as nothing but a giant real estate opportunity. But there are places - and people - that remind us that the most precious things in life aren't for sale at any price.

Even if you do put your name on them in giant gold letters.

Chapter 33

When Someone Wanted Their Canal Back

During his inaugural address, Trump vowed to "take back" the Panama Canal from Panama, suggesting he might use military force and accusing Panama of breaking promises and letting China control the waterway.

****

Hello dearies! The strangest thing happened at our history club meeting. Karen (you remember Karen—she still thinks adding a tiny American flag to anything makes it better) was all excited about the news that we might "take back" the Panama Canal.

"Take it back?" I asked, pausing in my pouring of coffee. "Like taking back a Christmas present you gave someone twenty-five years ago?"

Well! Karen got so worked up she put three sugars in her coffee instead of her usual two. "But we built it!" she said. "We paid for it!"

Harold looked up from his newspaper. "Like how we 'built' that nice sunroom on our old house on Maple Street? Funny, I don't recall the new owners asking our permission to repaint it."

You know what this reminds me of? When our old neighbors moved away but kept driving by their former house, complaining about every little change the new family made to "their" garden. Finally, Mrs. Peterson from next door said, "It's funny how hard it is for some folks to understand the meaning of the word 'former.'"

"But it's different," Karen insisted. "That canal is important!"

"Yes," I said, reaching for the coffee pot, "I imagine it's particularly important to Panama, seeing as how it runs right through their country and all."

The morning paper on Harold's lap had a big headline about making the canal "American" again. I couldn't help wondering if the water flowing through it had any opinions about its nationality.

(Though I notice nobody's suggesting we give Manhattan back to the Dutch, even if they did build the first roads.)

Chapter 34

When Countries Became Shopping Items

Hello dearies! I've been thinking about this business of trying to buy countries like they're properties in that Monopoly game Harold keeps in the hall closet. First Greenland, then talking about "taking back" the Panama Canal, and now I hear some folks are joking about Albania feeling left out of all this attention.

"Harold," I said while reading the morning paper, "remember when that real estate developer kept trying to buy up all the houses on Maple Street? How every time someone said no, he'd just move on to the next house?"

Harold lowered his newspaper. "Some folks think everything's for sale," he said. "Even things that were never on the market to begin with."

You know what this reminds me of? When that fancy new country club opened up across town. Suddenly our little golf course started putting up signs about being "just as good" and "worth noticing too." As if being overlooked by the wealthy somehow made them less valuable.

The thing about treating countries like properties in a game is that pretty soon everybody starts measuring their worth by whether someone's trying to buy them or not. Rather backwards way of looking at things, if you ask me.

Harold says it's like that old saying about being careful what you wish for—though I suppose if you're Albania, watching someone try to buy Greenland and take Panama, you might start wondering what's wrong with your mountains.

I mentioned all this at bridge club, and Betty (still working on that eternal scarf) said something that made me think. "It's like those makeover shows," she said. "Suddenly everybody starts feeling bad about themselves just because nobody's trying to fix them."

The funny thing is, Betty's right. Here's Albania with its lovely mountains and history, probably feeling like the only house on the block that didn't get an offer during the real estate boom. Though if they'd asked me (which they didn't), I'd tell them some attention isn't worth getting, and some offers aren't worth receiving.

(Though between us, any country that's managed to stay off certain people's shopping lists might want to count their blessings. Rather like how our little golf course eventually realized being "overlooked" by the country club crowd wasn't such a bad thing after all.)

Chapter 35

When Someone Quit the Climate Club

On his first day in office, Trump announced the U.S. would withdraw from the Paris Climate Accord.

****

Hello dearies! I need to tell you about something that happened at the garden club. Mrs. Peterson brought in her gardening journals—thirty years of planting dates and first frosts. "Look," she said, pointing to the pages, "spring comes earlier every year, and winter comes later."

Right then, someone mentioned we're pulling out of that Paris climate agreement. "It's too expensive," they said. "Besides, why should we do anything if other countries might cheat?"

Well! That reminded me of when our neighborhood had to clean up Miller Creek. Every single family had to help, or it wouldn't work. If we'd all waited for everyone else to prove they were doing their part first, we'd still be looking at trash in the water.

"Harold," I said that evening, showing him the headline, "remember how Mr. Jenkins didn't want to help with the creek because he lived 'upstream' from the worst part?"

Harold lowered his newspaper. "Funny how some folks think they can opt out of a problem just because they don't like the solution."

The thing about climate is that it doesn't care about agreements or politics or whether we believe in it or not. Rather like that creek—the trash was there whether Mr. Jenkins believed in it or not.

I keep thinking about Mrs. Peterson's garden journals, watching the seasons shift one year at a time. Some changes happen so slowly you hardly notice until someone shows you thirty years of proof in faded ink.

Betty's been noticing it too. Her prize roses used to bloom right in time for the Fourth of July garden show. Now they're done by mid-June. "The flowers don't read calendars," she says, "they read weather." And the weather's telling them something's different.

You know what bothers me most? It's not just about today. Those garden journals I keep? They're not just for me. They're for Tommy and his children and their children after them. Though at this rate, I'm not sure what kind of gardening advice they'll need.

(Though I suppose some folks think if they just don't sign the agreement, tomorrow won't come. Rather like Tommy closing his eyes and thinking we can't see him stealing cookies.)

Chapter 36

When Someone Left the Health Club

On his first day in office, Trump ordered the United States to withdraw from the World Health Organization, cutting off America's role as the organization's largest supporter of global disease prevention programs.

****

Hello dearies! Something happened at my hospital volunteer shift that I just can't stop thinking about. You see, I was organizing the children's library cart (yes, hospitals have library carts—being sick is boring enough without having nothing to read), when Dr. Roberts came in looking more worried than I've seen him since the time Tommy tried to do a backflip off the jungle gym.

"They're pulling us out of the WHO," he said, slumping into a chair. When he saw my confused face, he explained it wasn't a question, but rather the World Health Organization—the folks who help countries work together to fight diseases.

Well! That's like quitting the neighborhood watch program because you live on the "safe" side of town. Disease doesn't check passports before crossing borders, anymore than that chicken pox Tommy brought home from summer camp checked if his sister wanted it too.

"Harold," I said that evening, "remember when they closed our little hospital's research department? Said we could just use the big city hospital's findings?"

Harold lowered his newspaper. "Some folks think they can save money by letting others do all the work. Until the moment they need help themselves."

You know what this reminds me of? Back when we had that measles outbreak in '63. Our little town didn't have enough medicine, but thankfully other places did. That's what working together means—helping each other when things get rough.

Dr. Roberts showed me a picture of their team in Africa, working with local doctors to stop Ebola. "Disease anywhere is a threat everywhere," he said. "You can't just wall it out."

I thought about that while restocking the library cart. About how every medical book on those shelves contains knowledge shared by doctors around the world. About how every cure we have came from people working together, not apart.

(Though I suppose some folks think if they just don't cooperate with other countries, diseases will politely stop at the border. Rather like thinking a "No Soliciting" sign stops hurricanes.)

Chapter 37

When America Stopped Helping Others

On January 24, 2025, Secretary of State Marco Rubio issued imme-diate "stop-work orders" on nearly all foreign assistance programs, halting aid to allies and vulnerable populations worldwide, with exceptions only for Israel and Egypt.

****

Hello dearies! The strangest thing happened at church yester-day. Our mission committee was all excited about the water pump we were going to install in that little village in Africa—until some-one read about the new order to freeze all foreign aid.

"But we already promised!" Sister Margaret said, her voice shak-ing. She's been writing to those villagers for months, watching their progress through pictures. "They've already dug the well."

Well! That's like telling Tommy to stop building his treehouse when he's up in the tree with a hammer. Except this isn't about a treehouse—it's about people waiting for clean water.

"Harold," I said while making breakfast, "remember when the mill closed and everyone in town pitched in to help those families? Imagine if halfway through, someone had said 'Sorry, helping is too expensive.'"

Harold lowered his newspaper. "Some folks think being the richest country means never having to share. Rather like being the richest family on the block and turning off your porch light on Halloween."

The mission board showed us pictures of all the projects now frozen—schools half-built, medical supplies sitting in warehouses, farmers waiting for promised seeds. Sister Margaret says it's like telling someone drowning that we need to review our water safety protocols first.

You know what bothers me most? These aren't just numbers on a paper—they're promises we made. Real people waiting for real help that we said we'd provide. Though I suppose some folks think promises only count if you can see the people you made them to.

"But we need to take care of our own first," someone said at coffee hour. As if kindness is a pie that runs out if you share it too widely. My grandmother always said the more you give, the more you have to give. She wasn't talking about money—she was talking about heart.

(Though I notice the order doesn't freeze aid to certain countries. Funny how some promises are more frozen than others.)

Chapter 38

When Friendship Got Expensive

On January 26, 2025, Trump threatened Colombia with 50% tariffs and visa sanctions if it didn't accept deportees on military planes, forcing the proud nation to capitulate within hours.

****

Hello dearies! The oddest thing happened at my coffee club meeting. Betty was telling us about her son who works at that specialty coffee import business downtown, and how worried he is about these new tariffs being threatened against Colombia.

"Fifty percent!" she said, nearly spilling her cup. "Just to force them to do what we want about deportations. It's like putting a gun to someone's head and calling it a negotiation."

Well! I haven't seen Betty this worked up since they tried to change the timing of her grandmother's funeral to accommodate the pastor's golf schedule.

"Harold," I said later, showing him the news, "isn't Colombia supposed to be our friend? Our ally?"

Harold lowered his newspaper. "Some folks think friendship means doing whatever they say. Rather like that boy in Tommy's class who only plays with kids who give him their dessert at lunch."

The thing about bullying is it doesn't get prettier just because you do it with tariffs instead of fists. Betty's son says some of these Colombian farmers they work with have been growing coffee for generations. Built their whole lives around being good partners to America. Now suddenly we're threatening to destroy their livelihood if their government doesn't bow to demands?

You know what this reminds me of? When our church council threatened to withhold funding from the youth group unless they changed their meeting time to suit the council's schedule. Sister Margaret stood up and said, "Since when do we call it Christian behavior to starve people into submission?"

Betty showed me pictures of the Colombian family her son stays with when he visits the coffee farms. "These are real people," she said, "not just numbers on a trade document."

(Though I notice how quick we are to hurt friends when we think we can get away with it. Rather like how some folks only show their true nature when they think nobody's watching.)

Chapter 39

When Someone Got Their Countries Confused

Asked about Spain's NATO contributions on his first day in office, Trump repeatedly insisted Spain was a BRICS nation, apparently unaware that the 'S' in BRICS stands for South Africa.

****

Hello dearies! The strangest thing happened at our international cooking class. Karen (you remember Karen—she thinks adding sour cream to anything makes it "European") was telling everyone about how Spain is part of some group called BRICS.

"It's Brazil, Russia, India, China, and Spain," she announced, spooning what she claimed was paella but looked suspiciously like rice with food coloring. "The president said so."

Well! I haven't been this confused since Tommy tried to convince me that pizza counts as a vegetable because of the tomato sauce.

"Karen," I said, as gently as one can while watching her add ketchup to rice, "are you sure about Spain? Because I'm pretty sure the 'S' stands for South Africa."

"Oh, Mildred," she said with that smile she uses when she thinks she knows better (usually right before something burns). "I think I know my geography. Spain is definitely in Europe."

When I told Harold about it later, he lowered his newspaper. "Some folks," he said, "think being certain is the same as being right."

You know what this reminds me of? When Karen insisted her "authentic Italian meatballs" were correct because she'd seen them on a can of Chef Boyardee. Some things aren't true just because someone important says they are.

The funny thing is, now half our cooking class is convinced Spain is in BRICS, and the other half is worried about South Africa finding out it's been replaced. Though I suppose if you say something wrong with enough confidence, some folks will believe it over someone saying something right with doubt.

Betty tried to help by bringing in her grandson's geography textbook, but Karen just said it was "outdated"—even though it was printed last year. "Things change," she insisted, adding more ketchup to her rice. "Spain's probably just better at being the 'S' than South Africa."

I couldn't help wondering what South Africa would think about all this. Though I suppose if you're going to mix up countries, you might as well go all the way—rather like how Karen's "traditional Spanish recipe" somehow includes both maple syrup and ranch dressing.

(Though I notice Karen's "Spanish" rice remained untouched at the potluck table. Some things you can't fix just by renaming them.)

Chapter 40

When Someone Looked for a Magic Faucet

As wildfires ravaged Southern California, Trump insisted there must be a "very large faucet" somewhere that could be turned on to send Canadian water to California, suggesting officials were simply refusing to use it.

****

Hello dearies! Something happened at the city council meeting that I just can't stop thinking about. They were discussing our water shortage when someone mentioned how the president thinks there must be a "very large faucet" somewhere that could just send Canadian water to California's wildfires.

"Harold," I said later, "remember when Tommy was little and thought there was a magic switch that made it rain?"

Harold lowered his newspaper. "Difference is, Tommy was five."

Well! I haven't heard anything this peculiar since Karen suggested we could solve the church basement flooding by leaving out more buckets. As if water problems were just about finding a big enough container.

You know what this reminds me of? When our neighbor Mr. Wilson tried to "redirect" his sprinkler system to water his whole yard at once. Ended up flooding his garage instead. Some things aren't solved by just turning handles.

Betty, who used to work for the water department, actually had to sit down when she heard about this magic faucet idea. "Thirty years managing water systems," she said, "and I never once found the 'make everything better' valve."

The thing about water is that it follows its own rules. Rather like how my garden hose doesn't reach any further just because I want it to. Though I suppose if you've never had to figure out how to make the water go where it needs to go, you might think it's all just a matter of finding the right tap.

I remember during the drought of '83 when folks thought we could just pipe in water from the Great Lakes. "Geography," our old science teacher Mrs. Harris used to say, "doesn't care about what would be convenient."

"But he's the president," someone said at the council meeting. "Surely he understands how water works?" Betty just smiled that smile she saves for when Karen announces she's improved a classic recipe. Some things you can't fix by adding more ingredients—or by looking for magical faucets.

(Though I notice nobody's suggested looking for a giant faucet to solve their own country club's irrigation problems. Funny how some solutions only sound good when they're someone else's responsibility.)

Chapter 41

When Experience Stopped Counting

On his first day in office, Trump issued an executive order reclassifying tens of thousands of federal employees under "Schedule F," stripping them of civil service protections and making them subject to firing without cause.

****

Hello dearies! I need to tell you about my friend Ellen who works at the FDA. She's been testing food safety there for thirty years—so long she can spot a problem just by the smell. Yesterday she called me in tears.

"They're making us all 'Schedule F,'" she said. When I asked what that meant, she explained they could now be fired without cause. Thirty years of experience protecting people from unsafe food, and suddenly it counts for less than whether you agree with the right people.

Well! That reminded me of when our new church council tried to replace Mrs. Peterson as choir director because she wouldn't switch to "more modern" hymns. Fifty years of music experience meant less than following the new agenda.

"Harold," I said while making dinner, "remember when they replaced all the experienced teachers at Tommy's school with cheaper new graduates? How long did it take before parents started complaining about falling test scores?"

Harold lowered his newspaper. "Some folks think loyalty matters more than knowing what you're doing. Until the moment they need someone who knows what they're doing."

You know what this reminds me of? When they decided the school cafeteria didn't need professional nutritionists anymore. "Anyone can make lunch," they said. Three weeks and two dozen upset stomachs later, they realized maybe experience counted for something after all.

Ellen says it's not just her department. Scientists who've spent decades keeping our water clean, safety inspectors who know every rivet in a bridge, financial experts who can spot a market crash coming—all of them could be replaced by people whose main qualification is agreeing with whoever's in charge.

"But they have to have some reason to fire people," Betty said at bridge club. Ellen just laughed, but it wasn't her happy laugh. "The reason will be whatever they want it to be."

The thing about experience is you don't know how much you need it until it's gone. Like when our new pastor decided we didn't need the old emergency committee during storm season. "We'll figure it out as we go," he said. Tell that to the flooded basement that the old committee knew to check every hour during heavy rain.

Chapter 42

When Night Watchmen Disappeared

On January 25, 2025, in the dark hours before dawn, the Trump administration fired approximately seventeen federal inspectors general, the independent watchdogs charged with preventing abuse of power.

****

Hello dearies! The strangest thing happened at our neighborhood watch meeting last night. Mr. Peterson, who's been our coordinator for fifteen years, told us the new homeowners' association wants to eliminate the program entirely. "Too expensive," they said. "Unnecessary oversight."

"But what about when Mrs. Wilkins' garage was broken into? Or the Jenkins' car?" someone asked.

"We've hired our own security firm," was the answer. Though nobody mentioned that the firm belongs to the HOA president's brother-in-law.

Well! That reminded me of what I read in the paper about all those inspector general folks being fired in the middle of the night.

Seventeen watchdogs, all sent packing in the dark hours before dawn. The very people whose job it is to make sure government is behaving properly.

"Harold," I said over breakfast, "isn't that like firing the night watchman because he keeps reporting break-ins?"

Harold lowered his newspaper. "Some folks," he said, "prefer darkness for certain kinds of work."

You know what this reminds me of? When Tommy was little and would unscrew the hall light bulb so we wouldn't see him sneaking cookies at midnight. As if darkness itself was permission.

The thing about watchdogs is they're only a problem if you're doing something that needs watching. Rather like how our old cat Whiskers only bothered Harold when he was trying to sneak extra bacon from the fridge.

I mentioned all this to Betty while we were volunteering at the library. She just shook her head. "First rule of getting away with something," she said, "get rid of anyone who might be watching." Turns out Betty used to work in bank security. Who knew?

What bothers me most is how they did it—in those quiet hours before dawn, when most folks are dreaming rather than watching. As if they knew what they were doing wouldn't stand up to daylight.

(Though I notice they keep the security cameras running at their own houses. Funny how some things need watching more than others.)

Chapter 43

When Fair Play Got Rewritten

On January 22, 2025, Trump rescinded Executive Order 11246, Lyndon Johnson's landmark 1965 directive that banned discrimination by federal contractors and required affirmative action, thereby dismantling a cornerstone of civil rights law.

****

Hello dearies! Something happened at our library board meeting that's still bothering me. You see, for years we've had this policy that our staff should reflect our community—all parts of it. It wasn't always that way. When I first joined the board, you'd have thought everyone in town looked exactly the same, which (as anyone who's been to our Fourth of July picnic knows) simply isn't true.

Well! Our new board chairman wants to end that policy. "Merit-based hiring only," he announced, as if the two things were somehow opposite. As if our current librarians—who speak five languages between them and created the most popular children's program in the county—weren't hired on merit.

It reminded me of what I read in the paper about the president canceling that old order requiring companies with government contracts to have fair hiring practices. Sixty years of progress erased with a signature.

"Harold," I said while sorting through recipe cards, "remember when Sarah couldn't get an interview at the bank until she used just her initials on the application? I thought we were past all that."

Harold lowered his newspaper. "Some folks," he said, "think the playing field is level just because they've had a smooth walk across it."

You know what this reminds me of? When Tommy's baseball coach insisted that letting the smaller kids have a turn at bat was "unfair" to the natural athletes. As if the game was only about winning, not about everyone getting to play.

The thing about opportunity is that it's like my zucchini plants—it doesn't spread itself evenly without a little help. Some spots in the garden get more sun, more water, better soil. Without some evening out, you end up with one enormous zucchini and a dozen that never had a chance.

Betty worked at that manufacturing plant for thirty years. "Before that order," she told me, "they wouldn't even let women apply for anything but secretarial jobs. Didn't matter that I could fix engines better than half the men they hired."

I've been thinking about that while making my lemon squares. About how some barriers aren't visible until you're the one trying to walk through them. About how some people think giving everyone a fair chance somehow takes something away from them.

(Though I notice the folks most upset about "merit-based" anything are often the same ones whose children mysteriously get summer internships at their golf buddies' companies.)

Chapter 44

When Justice Took a Timeout

On his third day in office, Trump's Justice Department ordered an immediate freeze on all civil rights litigation and signaled it would reconsider police reform agreements, including consent decrees addressing police brutality in Minneapolis and Louisville.

****

Hello dearies! I need to tell you about something that happened at the town council meeting. They were discussing that lawsuit about wheelchair access at the community center—you know, the one Betty's been fighting for since her accident. Suddenly, Mayor Jenkins announced they were "pausing" all such complaints until further notice. "Budget review," he called it.

"But people need to get into the building now," Betty said, wheeling herself forward. "Rights don't have a pause button."

Well! That got me thinking about what I'd read in the paper about the Justice Department freezing all civil rights cases. As if fairness and equal treatment were luxury items you could put on layaway until more convenient times.

"Harold," I said while watering my African violets (they're so temperamental, rather like certain politicians), "remember when they tried to 'pause' school integration back in the 60s? How many generations of children would have lost their chance at better education if we'd let that happen?"

Harold lowered his newspaper. "Some folks," he said, "think justice is something you can schedule at your convenience. Rather like how Karen thinks she can show up three hours late to potlucks."

You know what this reminds me of? When Tommy's school decided to "temporarily" cancel the special reading program. Three years later, children were still struggling, and "temporary" had somehow become permanent.

The thing about progress is it's like bread dough—it doesn't wait while you take a nap. It either rises or it falls. There's no pause button.

I've been thinking about that courthouse downtown, the one with "Equal Justice Under Law" carved right into the stone. Nowhere does it say "Equal Justice When We Get Around To It" or "Equal Justice If It's Convenient."

Betty says the hardest part isn't even fighting for her own access. It's explaining to her granddaughter why some people think certain rights can be put on hold while others are considered essential. How do you explain to a child that justice sometimes takes a "timeout"—but only for some people?

(Though I notice they didn't freeze the lawsuits protecting certain businesses from regulation. Apparently, some rights don't need to wait their turn.)

Chapter 45

When Diversity Got Packed Away

On his first day in office, Trump ordered the immediate closure of all federal Diversity, Equity, and Inclusion offices, suspended DEI staff, and banned DEI considerations in government hiring and training.

****

Hello dearies! Something happened at the school board meeting that I just can't stop thinking about. They announced they're eliminating the diversity program that Mrs. Rodriguez started five years ago. "Non-essential," they called it, which is a funny way to describe something that helped our town's children finally start seeing themselves in their own classrooms.

Well! It reminded me of what I read in the paper about closing all those diversity offices in the federal government. As if understanding different perspectives was some kind of luxury we couldn't afford.

"Harold," I said while sorting through family photos for Tommy's school project, "isn't it strange how a classroom full of different kinds of children is just called a classroom, but the moment you try to make sure they all feel welcome, it becomes 'political'?"

Harold lowered his newspaper. "Some folks," he said, "think acknowledging differences is the same as creating them."

You know what this reminds me of? When our garden club decided we didn't need a committee to help new members feel welcome anymore. "Everyone's naturally friendly," they said. Six months later, half the new gardeners had quit because nobody had bothered to learn their names or show them where the tools were kept.

The thing about diversity is it's like my flower garden—it doesn't thrive on its own without some care and attention. You can't just throw all the seeds in together and hope they'll sort themselves out. Some need more sun, some need more shade, some need special soil. Pretending they're all exactly the same doesn't help anything bloom.

I was looking through those old school yearbooks from when our children were young. Page after page of faces that all looked remarkably alike. Now when I visit Tommy's class, it's like seeing the whole world in one room. Somehow, that's considered a problem that needs solving rather than a gift that needs nurturing.

Karen from church (you know Karen—she thinks adding raisins to perfectly good potato salad is "inclusive cooking") says we're all just Americans and shouldn't need special programs. I asked her if that means we should cancel the special reading help Tommy gets for his dyslexia. After all, we're all just readers, aren't we? She didn't have much to say to that.

(Though I notice nobody's eliminating the special programs for "gifted" children. Apparently, some differences are worth acknowledging.)

Chapter 46

When Doctors Had to Whisper

On his first day in office, Trump ordered an unprecedented freeze on all external communications from health agencies including CDC, FDA, and NIH, while halting scientific grant reviews and research funding indefinitely.

****

Hello dearies! I need to tell you about something troubling that happened at our hospital volunteer meeting. Dr. Williams, who's headed the public health department for twenty years, told us they've been instructed not to share any information about the new flu strain without approval from the mayor's office first.

"But people need to know how to protect themselves now," I said. "The mayor doesn't even check his email on weekends!"

Dr. Williams just gave me this sad smile. "Sometimes, Mildred, the people who know aren't allowed to tell, and the people allowed to tell don't know."

Well! That reminded me of what I read in the paper about all those health agencies being told to stop sharing information. The

CDC, the FDA, the NIH—all those scientists suddenly needing permission to warn us about what's coming.

"Harold," I said while checking the thermometer in my oven (accuracy matters in baking, just like in science), "remember when Tommy had that terrible allergic reaction, and the emergency room doctor explained exactly what was happening and why? Imagine if she'd had to wait for someone's approval before telling us he needed epinephrine."

Harold lowered his newspaper. "Some folks," he said, "think controlling information is the same as controlling problems."

You know what this reminds me of? When our church roof started leaking, and the building committee decided the solution was to stop the janitor from putting out buckets where people could see them. As if hiding the evidence would somehow fix the roof.

The thing about science is it's rather like my recipe for yeast bread—it doesn't work any differently just because you decide not to look at it. The dough still rises, the disease still spreads, the climate still changes.

At the senior center, Mr. Jenkins (who worked at the county health department for thirty years) told me these agencies have been publishing their weekly reports for nearly a century—through wars, depressions, and every kind of political upheaval. "Science doesn't take sides," he said. "It just tells you what's coming, whether you want to hear it or not."

Karen from church says it's all about making sure information is "accurate" before sharing it. I asked her if she'd like her smoke detector to wait for approval before alerting her to a fire. She changed the subject to her award-winning (participation award, if we're being honest) peach cobbler.

(Though I notice nobody's stopping the weather service from warning about hurricanes headed toward certain golf resorts.)

Chapter 47

When Clean Air Became Optional

On his first day in office, Trump ordered the mass deletion of EPA regulations protecting air and water quality, reversing decades of environmental safeguards established through scientific study and public health research.

****

Hello dearies! Something happened at the town council meeting that's been troubling me all week. They voted to stop testing our local creek water. "Too expensive," they said. "Unnecessary red tape." This is the same creek, mind you, where Tommy and his friends catch minnows every summer.

When I asked about the factory upstream that used to dump who-knows-what until testing began, Councilman Jenkins just shrugged. "They've promised to be responsible," he said, as if promises cleaned water better than regulations.

Well! That got me thinking about what I read in the paper—how they're deleting all those environmental rules with a few keystrokes. Five years of scientific studies, public health research, careful measurement—all gone in the time it takes to delete an email.

"Harold," I said while watering my tomato plants (the ones that need clean air and water, just like people do), "remember when Miller's Pond turned that strange color before they started regulating what could go into it? The fish didn't get a vote on whether those rules were 'unnecessary.'"

Harold lowered his newspaper. "Some folks," he said, "think nature follows their politics. Rather like thinking gravity will make an exception if you vote against it."

You know what this reminds me of? When our church nursery decided hand-washing rules were "excessive bureaucracy." Three weeks and seventeen sick babies later, they suddenly decided maybe soap and clean water had some value after all.

The thing about pollution is it's rather like Karen's perfume—it doesn't stay where you put it. It travels through air and water, visiting places it wasn't invited and staying longer than welcome.

I've been thinking about my grandmother's garden journal from the 1930s. The dates when birds returned, when flowers bloomed, when the first freeze came. How different those dates are now. Nature keeps its own records, you see, no matter what records we choose to delete.

Mr. Peterson, who worked for the state environmental office before he retired, tells me it took decades to clean up our river after the paper mill closed. "Rules aren't just words on paper," he said. "They're the difference between water you can drink and water that makes you sick."

(Though I notice they're keeping all the regulations that protect property values around certain golf courses. Apparently some environments are worth more than others.)

Chapter 48

When Someone Wanted His Face on a Mountain

As Trump began his second term, MAGA congressional representatives revived his dream of adding his image to Mount Rushmore, an idea he had repeatedly endorsed during his first term.

****

Hello dearies! Something happened at our historical society meeting that I just can't stop thinking about. We were discussing where to put the portrait of our former mayor (the one who got caught using the town snow plow to clear his private driveway), and he sent a message suggesting we should replace the founding families' portraits with a much larger picture of himself.

"But this is a historical society," Mrs. Peterson said. "The point is to remember those who built something lasting, not those who... well."

Well! That reminded me of what I read in the paper about wanting to add a face to Mount Rushmore. As if those four presidents hadn't earned their place through preserving the Union, writing our founding documents, and building the nation through genuine achievement.

"Harold," I said while dusting our family photos (some things are worth preserving just as they are), "remember when Tommy wanted to add his handprints to your father's cement patio? The one your dad poured himself back in '52?"

Harold lowered his newspaper. "Some folks," he said, "think they can chisel themselves into history instead of earning their way there."

You know what this reminds me of? When Karen insisted the church cookbook should feature her picture on the cover instead of Mrs. Wilson's, even though Mrs. Wilson had created the cookbook tradition thirty years earlier. "But I'm making it better," Karen said, apparently forgetting that adding raisins to perfectly good recipes isn't the same as creating something of lasting value.

The thing about monuments is they're meant to remind us of what we aspire to be, not just who made the most noise while they were here. Rather like how my grandmother's portrait still hangs in our hallway—not because she demanded it, but because her quiet dignity and kindness left a mark that demands remembering.

I mentioned all this at our garden club meeting. Old Mr. Jenkins, who rarely speaks up anymore, suddenly found his voice. "I saw those presidents when I was a boy," he said. "Even then I understood it wasn't about their faces. It was about their deeds."

(Though I notice nobody's suggesting we chisel Karen's coconut cake recipe into stone for future generations. Some things, mercifully, are allowed to be forgotten.)

Chapter 49

When Pens Became Weapons

In his first two weeks in office, Trump transformed the presidential signing pen from an instrument of democracy into a weapon of destruction.

****

Hello dearies! The strangest thing happened at our library board meeting last night. We were all given beautiful new pens to approve the yearly budget, when Mrs. Peterson reminded us that the same pens would be used next month to sign the defunding notice for the children's reading program.

"Feels wrong somehow," she said, setting her pen down. "Like being asked to use your good kitchen knife to slash your neighbor's tires."

Well! That got me thinking about what I've been reading about all these presidential orders being signed, one after another, dismantling environmental protections, revoking healthcare, canceling civil rights initiatives—all with the same ceremonial pen that's supposed to build things up, not tear them down.

"Harold," I said while writing my weekly letter to our grand-children (some things should be written carefully, with thought behind each word), "isn't it something how the same pen that signs a love letter could also sign eviction notices?"

Harold looked up from his crossword puzzle. "Some folks," he said, "never consider that tools reveal the heart of whoever holds them."

You know what this reminds me of? When our church got that beautiful new piano. Pastor Johnson was so proud until his son started playing those aggressive war-themed video game tunes on it during coffee hour. Same instrument, entirely different message.

The thing about pens—or any tools, really—is they don't have opinions about what they're used to do. My grandmother's fountain pen wrote both her wedding vows and, years later, the difficult letter disowning her brother after he betrayed the family. Same pen, but you can guess which one kept her awake at night.

I keep thinking about those pens we watch on television, signing order after order with such flourish. Gold-plated, shiny, important-looking things. I wonder if they ever wish they could run dry at exactly the right moment, or somehow make their ink invisible when what they're being asked to write goes against everything America is supposed to stand for.

(Though I notice they never seem to run out of ink when signing tax breaks for certain golf course owners. Funny how some pens are more cooperative than others.)

Chapter 50

When America Made Its Choice

Hello dearies.

I've been sitting at my kitchen table for a very long time today. No lemon squares cooling on the windowsill. No dough being kneaded. Just me, my thoughts, and the morning paper with those election results staring back at me.

"Harold," I said, my voice quieter than usual, "what do you say to a friend who keeps choosing the thing that hurts them?"

Harold set down his newspaper completely. We sat in silence, the kind that falls when words seem too small for the moment.

You know, when Tommy was little, he once chose to put his hand right on the stove after I'd warned him it was hot. The burn wasn't serious, thank heavens, but his tears weren't just from pain—they held confusion too, like he couldn't understand how something he'd chosen could hurt so much.

But Tommy was five. America is nearly 250 years old.

The thing about choices is they tell us something about who we are. Like when our church had to decide whether to spend money fixing the roof or installing a fancy new sign out front. They chose the sign, then acted surprised when rain poured in during Easter service. Some choices reveal priorities we might not want to admit, even to ourselves.

I keep thinking about my grandmother's quilt that hangs in our guest room. Each square tells a story—some beautiful, some painful, some complicated. America feels like that quilt right now. All these different pieces, somehow stitched together, with a pattern that's hard to make out when you're looking at just one square.

But a quilt doesn't stitch itself. Someone has to decide which pieces go where, which stories deserve telling.

What troubles me most isn't just the choice we made. It's that we made it with our eyes wide open. We saw the lies, the cruelty, the disregard for anything beyond self-interest. And we chose it anyway.

I don't have a cute story to make this better. No church social mishap or baking disaster that tidies up with a life lesson. Sometimes there's just the hard truth that we are what we choose to be, and we've chosen this.

The sun will still rise tomorrow. I'll probably make those lemon squares after all. Life continues, as it must. But something has changed, and I think it's happened inside us.

"We'll get through this," Harold said finally, reaching across the table for my hand.

I nodded, because what else can you do? But whether we'll be the same America on the other side—that's the question that keeps me awake at night.

Appendix:
Mildred's Lemon Squares

A Life in Lemon Squares

Hello dearies!

I suppose if we've come this far together, it's only right that I share the recipe that's been mentioned so often in these pages. But first, a little history about these lemon squares and me.

It started with my grandmother's recipe box. Not the fancy painted one she kept on the kitchen counter for company to see, but the battered tin one she kept tucked in the drawer by the sink. That's where the real treasures were. When she passed, my mother gave me that box, and tucked inside was a faded index card simply titled "Sunshine Squares."

My first attempt was... well, let's just say the lemon curd separated and the crust had the consistency of roof shingles. Harold (we were newlyweds then) ate three anyway and claimed they were delicious. That man has many virtues, but honesty about my early baking wasn't among them.

Over the years, I've made these squares for every occasion imaginable. They've celebrated births and comforted at funerals. They've welcomed new neighbors and said goodbye to old friends. They've been served at church socials, school fundraisers, and once, memorably, at the governor's mansion when our garden club won the state beautification award.

Yes, they've won ribbons at the county fair (seven blue, three red, and one we don't speak of from the year I experimented with less sugar). But the real prize has been watching faces light up when the plate is passed. In a world that grows more complicated by the day, there's something reassuring about the simple perfection of butter, sugar, and lemons coming together just right.

The secret? It's not in any particular ingredient or technique, though the zesting (never just juice!) matters tremendously. The real secret is in the making. Lemon squares need patience. They need attention. They need care. Rather like democracy itself, I suppose.

Through the years, I've learned you can tell a lot about people by how they approach my lemon squares. Some dive right in, trusting the experience will be worth the sticky fingers. Others nibble cautiously at the edges. Karen insists they need nutmeg, of course, but we've learned to smile and nod.

When Tommy was little, he'd always save the squares I packed in his lunch for last, "so the good part of lunch lasts longer," he explained. That boy understood something important even then—sometimes the sweet things in life deserve to be savored.

So here it is, dearies. Not just a recipe for lemon squares, but for a small moment of brightness in whatever darkness you may find yourself. Make them, share them, and remember that even in the sourest times, we can still create something sweet.

Mildred's Perfect Lemon Squares

For the Shortbread Crust:

- 1 cup (2 sticks) unsalted butter, at room temperature
- ½ cup granulated sugar
- 2 cups all-purpose flour
- ¼ teaspoon salt
- 1 teaspoon pure vanilla extract

For the Lemon Filling:

- 6 large eggs
- 2½ cups granulated sugar
- 1 tablespoon lemon zest (from about 2 lemons)
- 1 cup freshly squeezed lemon juice (from about 6-8 lemons)
- 1 cup all-purpose flour
- Powdered sugar, for dusting

Instructions:

1. Preheat your oven to 350°F. Line a 9x13-inch baking pan with parchment paper, leaving some overhang on the sides to help you lift the squares out later. (A little butter

on the pan helps the parchment stay put.)

2. For the crust: In a large bowl, cream together the butter and sugar until light and fluffy, about 3 minutes. Add the flour, salt, and vanilla, and mix just until combined. The dough will be crumbly.

3. Press the dough evenly into the bottom of your prepared pan. (A flat-bottomed measuring cup helps get it nice and even.) Bake the crust until just barely golden at the edges, about 15-18 minutes.

4. While the crust bakes, make the filling: In a large bowl, whisk together the eggs and sugar until smooth. Add the lemon zest, lemon juice, and flour, whisking until completely combined. No lumps allowed!

5. When the crust comes out of the oven, pour the filling over the hot crust. Return the pan to the oven and bake until the filling is set and doesn't jiggle in the center, about 20-25 minutes.

6. Allow the bars to cool completely in the pan on a wire rack. This is important—patience, dearie! Once cool, refrigerate for at least 2 hours before cutting.

7. When ready to serve, lift the bars out using the parchment paper overhang. Cut into squares with a clean knife (wiping between cuts gives you prettier edges). Dust generously with powdered sugar just before serving.

These keep beautifully in the refrigerator for up to 5 days, though they've never lasted that long in my house. For gifting, I like to place them in single layers separated by waxed paper.

Remember, the zest makes all the difference—that's where the brightest lemon flavor lives. And sifting the powdered sugar through a fine-mesh strainer gives that perfect snowy finish that makes everyone smile even before the first bite.

Sharing optional, but recommended. Even with Karen.

Also by Barry Robbins

About the author

B arry hails from Philadelphia and built a career with a promi-
nent international accounting firm, taking him to New
York, Washington, D.C., and San Francisco before a new chapter
brought him to Finland. He and his Finnish wife adopted two
daughters from China, and their family lived in Helsinki for twelve
years before he returned to the U.S., now calling Florida home. His
years in Finland gave him a new lens through which to view life in
America.

Barry's literary work blends satire, history, and political analysis.
Known for his Trump satires, including "The Weave", he's earned
three gold medals for his sharp wit. His curiosity also led to the
Ethereal Bar, a magical place where legends of history stop by for
poignant interviews.

Barry's most recent works reveal a thoughtful turn: "Trump and
the Soul of the Nation" examines the effect of the Trump years
through 2024 on what it means to be American, while "Voices of the Civil War", "Voices of the American Revolution", and
"Voices of Vietnam" bring an immersive, personal lens to these
tumultuous periods. His recent book "NO! a response to donald
j. trump" is exactly that. With a knack for balancing wit and in-
sight, Barry's writing invites readers to explore history from new,
intimate perspectives.